毕淑敏
双语美文

A Bilingual Edition of
Beautiful Stories
by Bi Shumin

U0725848

风不能把阳光打败

Wind Cannot Blow Away Sunlight

毕淑敏 著

朱虹 刘海明 译

GUANGXI NORMAL UNIVERSITY PRESS
广西师范大学出版社
· 桂林 ·

风不能把阳光打败
FENG BUNENG BA YANGGUANG DABAI

出版统筹：张俊显
品牌总监：耿　磊
选题策划：耿　磊
责任编辑：王芝楠
助理编辑：韩杰文
美术编辑：卜翠红　刘冬敏
营销编辑：杜文心　钟小文
责任技编：李春林

图书在版编目（CIP）数据

风不能把阳光打败：汉、英 / 毕淑敏著；朱虹，刘
海明译．—桂林：广西师范大学出版社，2020.1
　（毕淑敏双语美文）
　ISBN 978-7-5598-2394-6

Ⅰ．①风…　Ⅱ．①毕…②朱…③刘…　Ⅲ．①散文集－
中国－当代－汉、英　Ⅳ．①I267

中国版本图书馆 CIP 数据核字（2019）第 273114 号

广西师范大学出版社出版发行
（广西桂林市五里店路 9 号　邮政编码：541004）
　网址：http://www.bbtpress.com
出版人：黄轩庄
全国新华书店经销
保定市中画美凯印刷有限公司印刷
（保定市西三环 1566 号　邮政编码：071000）
开本：880 mm×1 350 mm　1/32
印张：6　　字数：120 千字
2020 年 1 月第 1 版　　2020 年 1 月第 1 次印刷
印数：0 001~6 000 册　　定价：39.80 元

如发现印装质量问题，影响阅读，请与出版社发行部门联系调换。

在书中温暖相遇

几年前，广西师范大学出版社出版了我的一套书。在这套书里，我写了自己在遥远西藏的往事，写了当医生的难忘经历，写了担当心理医生时听到的故事和引发的思考……

书是缔造心灵的塑形工具。东方文化中，心并不单单指那个解剖学上的泵血器官，而是汇聚每个人的品格情操的智慧之海。有一颗仁慈之心，会爱世界爱他人爱生活，爱自身也爱大家。有一颗自强之心，会勤学苦练百折不挠，宠辱不惊大智若愚。有一颗尊严之心，会珍惜自然善待万物。有一颗流量充沛羽翼丰满的心，会乘上幻想飞船，抚摸众星的翅膀。

我遇到了朱虹老师，她就是拥有这样一颗多彩之心的睿智长者。很高兴她喜欢我书中的文字。

最初，朱虹老师想挑一些篇章翻译，作为礼物送给远在大洋彼岸的孙女外孙女们珍藏。广西师大出版社的编辑获悉这个想法，郑重邀请朱虹和刘海明老师，将本套书全部翻译出来。

这不是轻易可完成之事，是颇为繁复艰辛的工程。朱虹老师已年近90，是中国社科院德高望重的英美文学研究专家，也是一位把我国很多当代文学作品翻译介绍到国外的杰出翻译家。长期生活在国外的刘海明老师造诣高超文采斐然，和朱虹老师相得益彰珠联璧合。两位老师以醇厚学养和丰富经验，深思熟虑地将这些文字，按照英语思维方式和阅读风格，给予精彩转化，赋予它们以另外一种语言表达的鲜活生命。

补充一个小插曲。我的散文"精神的三间小屋"，被选入2018年教育部审定的全国义务教育语文教科书九年级上册。刘海明老师加班加点，将这篇文章翻译出来，收入本套书，真是雪中送炭。

面对这套双语书，我心中充盈知遇之恩和感念之情，在此向所有付出心血的老师们深表谢意！

人生是砥砺向前且充满顿挫的历程，不时筋疲力尽茫然四顾。这本小书的故事和它的成书过程，让我又一次相信，行程中有不期而至的风雨，更有美好温暖的巧遇。朱虹、海明老师和我在文字中结识，现在，我期待着——我们和你——亲爱的读者，在书中相逢。

之后，让咱们再次充满信心地出发！

2019年11月5日

When We Meet Inside a Book

A few years ago, Guangxi Normal University Press published a collection of my stories. In them, I wrote about the years I spent in remote Tibet, my unforgettable experience working as a physician, and stories and musings I gathered as a counseling psychologist.

Works of literature help shape our heart. In Eastern cultures, the heart is the sea of wisdom that nurtures our character, other than a mere organ anatomically responsible for pumping blood through the body. It is with the kind heart that one loves the world, others and life; love of oneself and all people. It is with the hardy, aspiring heart that one strives on, never giving up, and is wise, artless and unflappable. It is with the dignified heart that one cherishes nature and is kind to all creatures great and small. It is with the heart brimful of confidence that one floats on wings of imagination, touching the stars.

Then I met Zhu Hong, an erudite elder with such an unfailingly rich heart, and was most delighted that she liked the stories of this collection.

Initially, Zhu Hong had planned to translate a selection of them as a gift to be held dear by her granddaughters across the ocean. However, when the editorial staff of Guangxi Normal University Press learned about this, they decided to invite Zhu Hong and Liu Haiming to translate the entire collection into English.

It was no small undertaking, a project requiring much dedication. Zhu Hong, in her late eighties, is a venerated scholar in the field of English and American Literature with the Chinese Academy of Social Sciences. She is also noted for her incomparable translations of outstanding works of modern Chinese literature, bringing them to a wider international audience. Liu Haiming, an accomplished translator having studied and worked extensively abroad, collaborated with Zhu Hong on this project. The two scholar-translators pored over the Chinese texts and managed to bring out the spirit of the original, and give life to the stories in the English language in all its beauty and flexibility.

Incidentally, my essay "Three Little 'Rooms' for Your Soul" was selected for the 2018 edition of the Ministry of Education-approved high school textbook for Chinese Language and Literature, for the first semester of the ninth year of National Compulsory Education. Beavering away, Liu Haiming had it timely translated for inclusion in the present collection.

As this bilingual collection was ready for printing, I felt most grateful for our privileged connection. My thanks go to all who have put all the hard work into its publication.

Life is a journey, with inevitable challenges and setbacks, which, at times, can wear you out, and loneliness captures you. Yet, for all the storms out of the blue, there are also fortuitous, heartening encounters along the way—a belief borne out by the stories in this collection and its publication. Zhu Hong, Haiming and I met in the pages of these stories, and now I look forward to our encounter with you, dear readers, in this little collection.

Then, brimful of confidence again, we will journey on!

Bi Shumin, November 5, 2019

contents
目 录

contents
目 录

自信第一课

　　一九七二年的一天，领导通知我速去乌鲁木齐报到，新疆军区军医学校在停顿若干年后第一次招生，只分给阿里军分区一个名额，首长经过研究讨论决定让我去。

　　按理说，我听到这个消息应该喜出望外才是。且不说我能回到平地，吸足充分的氧气，让自己被紫外线晒成棕褐色的脸庞"休养生息"，就是从学习的角度讲，"重男轻女"的部队能够把这样宝贵的唯一的名额分到我头上，也是天大的恩惠了。但是在记忆中，我似乎对此无动于衷，也许是雪山缺氧把大脑冻得迟钝了。我收拾起自己简单的行李，从雪山走下来，奔赴乌鲁木齐。

一九六九年，我从北京到西藏当兵，那种中心和边陲的，文明和狂野的，优裕和茹毛饮血的，高地和凹地的，温暖和酷寒的，五颜六色和纯白的……一系列剧烈反差让我的心发生了沧海桑田般的变化。距离死亡咫尺之遥，面对冰雪整整三年，我再也不是当初那个天真烂漫的城市女孩，内心已变得如同喜马拉雅山万古不化的寒冰般苍老。我不会为了什么突发事件和急剧的变革而大喜大悲，只会淡然承受。

入学后，从基础课讲起，用的是第二军医大学的教材，教员由本校的老师和新疆军区总医院临床各科的主任、新疆医学院的教授担任。记得有一次，考临床病例的诊断和分析，要学员提出相应的治疗方案。那是一个不复杂的病案，大致的病情是由病毒引起重度上呼吸道感染，病人发烧、流涕、咳嗽、血象低，还伴有一些阳性体征。我提出方案的时候，除了采用常规的治疗外，还加用了抗生素。

讲评的时候，执教的老先生说，凡是在治疗方案里使用了抗生素的同学都要扣分。因为这是一个病毒感染的病例，抗生素是无效的。如果使用了，一是浪费，二是造成抗药性，三是无指征滥用，四是表明医生对自己的诊断不自信，一味追求保险系数……老先生发了一通火，走了。

后来，我找到负责教务的老师，讲了课上的情况，对他说，我就是在方案中用了抗生素的学员。我认为那位老先生的讲评有不完全的地方，我觉得冤枉。

教务老师说，讲评的老先生是新疆最著名的医院的内科主任，他的医术在整个新疆是首屈一指的。他是权威，讲得很有道理。你有什么不服的呢？

我说，我知道老先生很棒。但是具体问题要具体分析。他提出的这个病例并没有说出就诊所在的地理位置。比如要是在我的部队，在海拔五千米以上的高原，病员出现高烧等一系列症状，明知是病毒感染，一般的抗生素无效，我也要大剂量使用。因为高原气候恶劣，病员的抵抗力大幅度下降，很可能合并细菌感染。如果到了临床上出现明确的感染征象时才开始使用抗生素，那就晚了，来不及了。病员的生命已受到严重威胁……

教务老师沉默不语。最后，他说，我可以把你的意见转告给老先生，但是，你的分数不能改。

我说，分数并不重要。您听我讲完了看法，我已知足了。

教室的门开了，校工闪了进来，搬进来一把木椅子摆在讲案旁，且侧放。我们知道，老先生又要来了。也许是年事已高，也许是习惯，总之，老先生讲课的时候是坐着的，而且要侧着坐，面孔永远不面向学生，只是对着有门或有窗的墙壁。不知道他这是积习，还是不屑于面对我们，或是有什么难言之隐。

这一次，老先生反常地站着。他满头白发，面容黢黑如铁，身板挺直如笔管，让我笃信了他曾是医官一说。

老先生目光如锥，直视大家，音量不大，但在江南口音中运了力道，话语中就有种清晰的硬度了。他说，听说有人对我的讲评有意见，好像是一个叫毕淑敏的同学。这位同学，你能不能站起来，让我这个当老师的也认识你一下？

我只有站起来。

老先生很注意地看了我一眼，说，好。毕淑敏，我认识你了，你可以坐下了。

说实话，那几秒钟真把我吓坏了。不过，有什么办法呢？说出的话就像注射到肌肉里的药水一样，是没办法抠出来的。

全班寂静无声。

老先生说，毕淑敏，谢谢你。你是好学生，你讲得很好。你的话里有一部分不是从我这儿学到的，因为我还没有来得及教给你那么多。是的，作为一个好的医生，一定不能全搬书本，一定不能教条，要根据具体的情况决定治疗方案。在这一点上，你们要记住，无论多么好的老师，也不可能把所有的规则都教给你们。我没有去过毕淑敏所在的那个五千米高的阿里，但是我知道缺氧对人的影响。在那种情况下，她主张使用抗生素是完全正确的。我要把她的分数改过来……

我听到教室里响起一阵轻微的欢呼。因为写了抗生素治疗的不仅我一个，很多同学都为这一改正而欢欣。

老先生紧接着说，但在全班，我只改毕淑敏一个人的分数。你们有人和她写的一样，还是要被扣分。因为你们没有说出她那番道理，是知其然而不知其所以然。你现在再找我说也不管事了，即使你是冤枉的也不能改。因为就算你原来想到了，但对上级医生的错误没敢指出来。对年轻的医生来说，忠诚于病情和病人，比忠实于导师要重要得多。必要的时候，你宁可得罪你的上司，也万万不能得罪你的病人……

这席话掷地有声。事过这么多年，我仍旧能够清晰地记得老先生如锥的目光和舒缓但铿锵有力的语调。平心而论，他出的那道题目是要求给出在常规情形下的治疗方案，而我竟从某个特殊的地理环境出发，并苛求于他。对一个初出茅庐的年轻人的不够全面的异议，老先生表现出了虚怀若谷的气量和真正的医生应有的磊落品格。

真的，那个分数对我来说完全不重要，重要的是我在此番高屋建瓴的话语中悟察到了一个优等医生的拳拳之心。

我甚至有时想，班上同学应该很感激我的挑战才对。因为没过多长时间，老先生就因为身体的关系不再给我们讲课了。如果不是我无意中创造了这个机会，我和同学们的人生就会残缺一段非常宝贵的教诲。

我的三年习医生涯，在我的生命中是一个重大的转折。我从生理上洞察人体，也从精神上对自己有了更多的信任。我知道了我们的灵魂居住在怎样的一团组织之中，也知道了它们的寿命和局限。如果说在阿里的时候我对生命还是模模糊糊的敬畏，那么，老师的教诲使我确立了这样的观念：一生珍爱自身，并把他人的生命看得如珠似宝，全力保卫这宝贵而脆弱的珍品。

My First Lesson in Self-Confidence

One day in 1972, I was informed by my superiors that I had been chosen for a spot at the medical school of Xinjiang Military Region, reopened after being closed for several years. The entire Ngari Military Sub-region was allowed only one place and I was given the opportunity, following a decision by the sub-regional command. I was to present myself at the school in Urumqi as soon as possible.

I should have been overjoyed. It was such a boon, the only spot being given to me, all the more unusual because it was in the military where the overwhelming majority were males. I would be able to pursue medical training, not to mention going to an area at a lower elevation, breathing enough oxygen and getting a break from extreme UV exposure on the highlands that had given me my russet, sunburned complexion. Yet, I recall not even mild excitement. Perhaps my mind had gone numb thanks to the utter cold and thin air on the highlands. I gathered my few belongings and travelled without delay to Urumqi, bidding my quiet farewell to the snowy mountains.

I had first arrived in Tibet back in 1969, having been enlisted in the army. Coming from Beijing, I was stunned by the stark, harsh nomadic way of life, the extreme cold, dizzying elevation and raw whiteness that contrasted sharply to the city's cultured manners, comfort, flat terrain, mild weather and gaudy colours. I was changed profoundly. Having been to the edge of life, with death being never far away and in the presence of the great snowy mountains for the full of three years, I was no longer the naïve, excitable town girl. I became more attuned to the timelessness of the ancient glaciers high in the Himalayas. I could take any change that came out of the blue with fortitude and aplomb, neither walking on air nor plunging into glum. So I reacted to the news of the medical school.

We started with the foundation courses and were taught by a stellar cast of instructors that included chief physicians and department heads of the General Hospital of Xinjiang Military Region and professors from Xinjiang Medical University, in addition to the faculty of our own school. We used standard textbooks published by the Second Military Medical University. I recalled an exam that involved diagnosis and analysis of certain clinical cases. We were asked to propose treatment for a relatively uncomplicated case — severe infection in the upper respiratory tract caused by viruses, with symptoms of fever, a running nose, coughing, a low white blood cell count, and other pathological signs. I proposed a course of medication that included antibiotics.

When giving his feedback, the old preceptor

fumed before leaving the classroom, "Points will be deducted for anyone who suggested antibiotics for this case. They don't work on viral infections. Any such application is a waste, and improper medication without indication, may cause drug resistance and that's a sign of self-doubt in the physician who opted to err on the side of caution ... "

"I am the one who proposed the use of antibiotics," I later told the academic dean when I went to lodge a complaint. "I didn't agree with the preceptor's comments. I felt wronged."

"He is the chief physician of the best-known hospital in Xinjiang and the best in the field in our region; an unrivalled authority to be exact. I don't see anything wrong with his comments. Why did you feel wronged?" the academic dean asked.

"I know his great reputation," I said. "But about the case cited in the exam, he didn't specify any location. Should it have occurred in my army unit in an area more than 5,000 meters above sea level, I would go with a course of medication including large doses of antibiotics, knowing full well it is viral infection, if the patient has a high fever in addition to other symptoms. As high altitudes weaken the body's defences, the patient may well develop bacteria-related complications. By the time bacteria-caused infection becomes evident, it will be too late to use antibiotics. The patient's life would have been in danger ... "

The dean fell silent before finally saying, "I can pass on your feedback. However, I cannot change your score."

"I am content now that you've heard me out," I said. "The score is not that important."

When a school staff opened the classroom door and brought in a wooden chair, placing it sideways next to the instructor's desk, we knew our preceptor would be here again. Either because of age or out of habit, he always sat when giving lectures, facing the side of the room with the windows or the door, but never the class directly.

I had no clue if it was mere idiosyncrasy, or because of his disdain for the uninspiring class, or some other unspeakable secrets.

This time, however, he stood all the time. Straight as a ramrod, with a full head of grey hair and a swarthy face, he must have once been an army field doctor, so I was convinced.

Fixing the class with a steely stare, he said in a clipped southern accent, with an unequivocal firmness, "I heard someone was not happy with the comments I made last time. Will this person by the name of Bi Shumin stand up so that I know who you are?"

I could only rise to my feet.

"Right, I see you now, Bi Shumin. You can sit down," the preceptor said, after giving me an intense look.

To be honest, I was scared stiff in those few seconds. Well, what's done is done. I could not retract what I had said. No point fretting over spilled milk.

As an utter silence descended, the preceptor continued, "I must thank you, Bi Shumin. You are a good student and

I commend you for your candour. I didn't teach you all that and I have yet to come to the point you raised. True, you should not be dogmatic and bookish if you want to be a great doctor. You have to take into account specific conditions of the patient. Remember also no teacher can give you all the answers. I have never been to Ngari where Bi Shumin had been stationed, at an elevation of 5,000 meters above sea level. However, I know the effects of low levels of oxygen on patients. Her recommendation of antibiotics in that context was correct. I will change the score I gave her ... "

There was a small wave of cheers in the classroom, for there must have been others who had also suggested antibiotics and now felt relieved and happy.

However, the preceptor added, "I will change Bi Shumin's score only. Some of you may have put down the same recommendation. Yet I am not sure if you had the same assumption. Even if you did, you didn't object when your recommendation was overruled. Don't try telling me now so as to have your scores changed. A medical student must learn that it is far more important to be truthful to your patient than to please your preceptor. You should always act in the best interests of your patients even if it means rousing the ire of your supervisors..."

The preceptor's words were firm and uncompromising. After all these years, I remember still his stern, penetrating gaze and his gentle, yet firm, resonant voice. In all fairness, the case cited in the exam called for a course of therapy under normal circumstances. But I argued accusatorily in my own defence by citing circumstances peculiar to a unique region. In contrast, he showed great tolerance and munificence true to a fine doctor, accommodating the partial opinion of a self-serving green horn.

I was touched by the honesty and devotion of a superior medical practitioner, shown in his principled and inspiring words. Getting my score changed or not already seemed frivolous.

My classmates should have all been grateful to me, for shortly after the episode, the preceptor stopped giving us lectures for good due to health reasons. Had I not inadvertently created the occasion by voicing my objection, we would all have missed a lesson that was to be of tremendous value to us in our lives later.

Three-years of medical school brought a major change to my life. With greater knowledge of human physiology, I came to have more confidence in myself. With an understanding of the organic matters in which our soul resides, I learned the extent of their life and their limitations. While I began to have a vague reverence for life when I was in Ngari, Tibet, it was my preceptor at the medical school who helped me develop such a conviction: cherish life, live it well, value that of others, too, and do what it takes to save and protect life — fragile, yet precious above all else.

请听凭内心

根据心理学的原则，人的行为动机无限多样，具有不可猜测性。所以，不必时时刻刻知道别人怎么想，你只要清楚地知道自己是怎样想的，就相当不错了。

也许你要说，知己知彼百战百胜嘛！这句古话固然不错，但那充其量只是一个充满了浪漫主义的想象，有谁能在一生中百战百胜？既然不可能，那么也只有听凭内心，况且人生也不是战场，有什么必要在和别人交往中，百战百胜呢？那是战争哲学，不是快乐的处世之道。

我们不能随随便便改变生命中最基本的事物，这就是我们的集体无意识。我们不能改变友爱，这是我们从远古到今天不至于灭亡的法宝之一。我们不能不歌颂勇敢，因为那是祖先的光荣，我们不是懦弱者的后代，不是，永远不是。我们必须珍视凌越一己生命之上的某些东西，因为正是它们，将我们和动物区分开来。我们只有爱好光明，不然我们会成为黑暗中的蛆虫……就这么简单，如果你想撼动某些精神的法则，只有你自己的灭失作为结局，而人类依然向前。

　　请消除对于生存之艰苦的怯懦。

　　我们有理由怕苦，怕太热，怕太冷，怕风沙，怕熊罴……总而言之，怕那些令我们不舒适的东西。

　　不过，所有的新发现中，都会有一些不熟悉的因子存在着，都会有风险和失败等着我们。消除这些恐惧的最简单的方式，就是不畏惧生存之艰苦。当我们的身体能够适应苦难的时候，我们的意志也往往会跟随。

Listen to Your Heart

Psychologists believe that human motivations are infinitely varied and unpredictable. Therefore, you needn't spend every waking hour trying to guess what others think. You will do yourself a great favour if you know clearly your own thinking.

You may retort by quoting the ancient sage, "Know your enemy and yourself, and you will not be imperilled in all battles." Well, that at best is a romantic aspiration. After all, who can be sure of victory in every battle they wage? So, let's get that out of the way; we must listen to our own inner voice. Life is not a war. Why should we always try to gain the upper hand in every interaction and engagement? The art of war has nothing to do with blissful living.

We cannot change the most fundamental of humanity — our collective subconscious. We cannot change our love of camaraderie — the secret to our species' survival since our primordial beginning. We glorify valour, for that is the name of our forebears; we are never, ever descendants of the weak and timorous. We cherish altruism, which transcends ego and separates us from other animals. We are drawn to the bright and virtuous, or else we are no different from worms in mildewy darkness ... If you attempt to resist such principles of the human spirit, you would be doomed while humanity marches on.

We should not fear hardships in life. We are rationally adverse to what makes us uncomfortable — too much hard work, too hot or too cold weather, the sandstorms, the bears that comes down from the mountain... Yet, nothing comes from nothing. When the living gets tough, the simplest solution is to face it head-on and tough it out. When our body is attuned to hardships, our resolve will be firmer, too.

自助者天助之

学会不怨天尤人，勇敢地负起自己应该负起的责任，这是一种美德，并且会给自己带来意想不到的礼物，那就是——你将一手造就自己的经历，为自己带来好运气。

我一直很相信这样一种说法：当你坚定地承担责任勇往直前的时候，天地万物好像听到了一个指令，会齐心协力地帮助你、提携你。于是，贵人也出现了，机会也在最不可能滋生的崖缝中，露出了细芽。

我有时自己也想不通，这不是迷信吗？天下万物怎么会听从一个指令呢？它们的耳朵在哪里？它们的听力如何？这个指令是什么人发出来的呢？它用的是何种语言？

想不通啊想不通！但现实中确实有这样的故事，我听到很多人这样说过，在充满了感动的同时，也充满了疑惑。想啊想，我终于理出了一点头绪。

那个帮你忙的指令，其实出自你的内心。一个人，如果他是积极向上永不妥协的，那么，他的一举一动一笑一颦，都会放射出这种不屈的信息。这就像香草就要发出烘烤般的酥香气息，拦也拦不住，堵也堵不了。所有经过他身边的人，都会看到这种灼热光华，如同走过夜明珠的身旁。

我坚信，很多人在内心里，是愿意帮助别人的。特别是这种帮助并不会带给自身重大损失的时候，很多人都愿意伸出友谊之手。

这种手，有的时候是一个机遇，给谁都是给，为什么不给一个让我们心生好感的人呢？为什么不给一个让人们心怀敬重的人呢？为什么不给一个具备美德的人呢？于是你就得到了它。

有的时候，援手是一个信息。因为你让对方感到愉悦，人在愉悦的时候就会浮想联翩。施助者的潜意识喜欢你，就想——也许这个消息对这个人会有益处呢？于是，它把这句话送到了主人的嘴边。很可能连主人都没有意识到这种好感和这条信息之间的关联，但勤快的潜意识就麻利地把事情给办妥了，没想到不经意间，这便成就了你的新生。

更多的时候，援手是一点小钱。这对有钱人算不得什么，对贫困中的人，却是天降甘露。你可能因为有了这一点小钱，而获得了转机，迎来了拐点。这对于施恩之人来说，很可能只是举手之劳。钱和钱的概念有时有天壤之别，用处也大相径庭，钱是会玩魔术的。

援手有的时候只是鼓励和关爱。虽然鼓励和关爱并不需要太大的付出，但人们只会鼓励那些和自己的人生大目标相投的人，会关爱和自己的爱好信仰相符的人。

一个人只有在光明磊落的时候，才会不避讳自己的奋斗目标，才会在很多不经意的瞬间显示出美德和惹人怜爱的细节。而这些，恰好具有打动人心的力量，奇迹就慢慢地显影了。

世界上的事，都是因人而异。对你难于上青天的事，对另外一些人不过是小菜一碟。所以，先锤炼你的人格和目标吧。当它们光彩照人的时候，机遇就在不知不觉中降临了。

这没有什么可神秘的，只要你像雏鹰，无数次张开翅膀，有一次正好刮过来了风，那是一股上升的气流。如果你蜷曲在巢中，无论刮过怎样的风，对你都只是寒冷。

Heaven Helps Those Who Help Themselves

Stop complaining about your ill-fortune or blaming others; have courage to take responsibility for yourself and your actions. It is a virtue to be cultivated and you will be surprised by its rewards — blessings of good luck and the power to shape your life.

I have always believed in the notion that he who strives finds his gods strive for him equally. He is truly blessed. Opportunities and "benefactors" crop up where they would otherwise be improbable, as if at his command.

I did have moments of doubt though: Isn't all this a bit too superstitious? How could all gods line up as if by some divine order? Do they have ears or eyes? Where does the order come from? In what language?

It makes little sense. Yet I have heard many talk about such experiences that they claim to be real. With a mixture of scepticism and inspiration, I thought long and hard before hitting upon my rationalization.

The power that commands the blessing of gods comes from you. If you have a positive mindset and unfailing tenacity, you are a bundle of energy, exuberant and indomitable. All in your presence feel the radiance of your spirit — irresistible, like the scent of roasting chestnuts — and in turn take on a glow themselves as if reflecting the beacon fire at night.

For although most of us are inclined to help, and many are ready to lend a hand, especially when it doesn't cost them much, whom to help is always a matter of choice. We help most heartily those who are veritably virtuous, who delight us and inspire our admiration. You will indeed be such a blessed person, if you strive.

Sometimes, help may come in the form of information.

Because you delight others, they take to you in spite of themselves. They may spontaneously mention things that will benefit you. Their partiality and affinity to you works efficiently at the subconscious level and, without their knowing it, the information they pass on may very well change your life.

More often, such help can be monetary, a small sum to the haves, a timely godsend to the have-nots. A small act of generosity, barely worth mentioning on the part of the giver, may bring a turnaround that changes your lot forever. There can be a world of difference as to how the haves and have-nots view and expend money. Money does work magic.

At other times, such help may be no more than words of encouragement or concern. We tend to show such support and care to the kindred spirits who share our values, beliefs and goals. Only when you are forthcoming and candid, not being evasive about your goals in life, can you earn others' support and encouragement. Your virtue and disarming personality shines through, in every endearing detail, when you are your true self, unguarded and unpretentious.

Asperity of adversity is relative. Your insurmountable travail may be easy as pie to someone else. So, be a better person and be purposeful. As you evolve into a stronger, more shining version of yourself, opportunity knocks without your imploring.

There is really nothing mystic in all this. A fledgling condor, spreading its wings tentatively, learns to catch the rising air and soar. You, too, have the power to make it happen. If you recoil, hiding in the nest, you will experience nothing but bitter chill as the wind starts to blow.

机遇是心灵的阅兵

在各行各业取得成功的人们，在拥有才情之外，一定还拥有强大的心灵。成功比试的不仅仅是才能，更重要的是韧性。即使没有公认的成功，也要有品尝幸福的能力，这就更取决于心灵的健全，而不仅仅是才能的显赫了。

才能这个东西，比较有办法弥补。只要不是那些需要才思铺天盖地喷如泉涌的事业，就可以用外力来加以补充。人家都知道"勤能补拙"的原则，都知道"笨鸟先飞"的故事，都记得"磨刀不误砍柴工"的诀窍，都会说"百分之一的才能，百分之九十九的汗水"之类的格言，这些都是补偿之法。

不过，世上的成功，除了才能之外，还有机遇。有人以为机遇是一种看不见摸不着的小概率事件，基本上和被闪电劈着差不多，这是误解。

机遇的降临，看起来好像取决于那个执掌机遇的人，领受者不过是被动地承接，其实不然。我们常常听到一个人不是为了名利而帮助别人，却不料那个被帮助的人将一个绝好的机会，赐予了帮助者。我们在羡慕此人轻而易举获得好运的时候，多半忘了他也许曾经这样帮助过很多人，绝大多数都无声无息地湮灭了，只有这一次金光灼灼。

有的人会不遗余力地学习各种知识。这些知识，分散开来，都是普通的学问和技能，无甚出奇。但是当它们密集地集中到一个人身上的时候，就显出了某种非同凡响的优势。

我认识一个小伙子，他学习了驾驶，学习了烹调，学习了英语，学习了会计，最后，还学习了擒拿格斗。怎么样？分门别类地看，都很平凡吧？可你想一想，一个会计，还会武功，英语熟练，开车又稳当，还做得一手好饭……他找到一个给某成功人士当贴身秘书的好工作，是不是顺理成章的事？

机遇其实是对人的心理素质的一次大阅兵。

你能不能抱定了前进的目标，持之以恒，在看不到希望的时候，不气馁不逃避，依然顽强地努力，乐观地积攒自己的力量和本领？

如果你真的能做到这些，机遇的概率就越来越大了。

Opportunity Knocks for the Prepared

In all walks of life, those who succeed not only have extraordinary talent but also a hardy soul. Success depends not only on one's talent but, more importantly, on resilience. You should appreciate how blessed you are, even if you have not succeeded by conventional definitions. To do that, you need a great heart in addition to talent.

It is possible to make up for a lack of talent. This holds true for any endeavour where dazzling, profuse creativity is not a prerequisite. We have all heard that "hard work can make up for a lack of natural talent and skills." Adages such as "The early bird gets the worm," "Honing hatchet does not slow woodcutting," and "Genius is one percent inspiration, ninety-nine percent perspiration" abound. They teach us how to overcome a lack of talent.

Beside talent, opportunity is also critical to success. Some are inclined to think opportunity is a rare gift, its probability as low as being struck by lightning, which is a misunderstanding. It may seem that an opportunity can only be received, never proactively sought, which is untrue. We hear stories of someone being blessed with a wonderful opportunity, given by the person he had selflessly helped before. As we envy his good fortune, we often forget his past acts of generosity. For one luminous instance of being blessed with an opportunity, many acts of generosity are done, though little known.

Some spare no efforts in equipping themselves with knowledge and skills of one kind or another, which make them exceptional, though each skill alone is quite commonplace.

I know such a young man who had learned to drive, cook, speak English, and do bookkeeping and kickboxing. He would be very ordinary if with only one of those skills. However, wouldn't you think it only natural for him to get the envied job of personal assistant to a highly successful personality, when he is a fine accountant with martial skills, speaks fluent English, drives safely and serves up nice dishes?

Opportunity knocks for the well prepared.

Do you have a clear goal and work with tenacity and perseverance? Do you persist, never get discouraged or give up when your dream seems beyond reach? Do you learn and acquire skills and get prepared with unfailing optimism? If you do all of these, the probability of your being blessed with opportunities will become much higher.

握紧你的右手

常见女孩郑重地平伸着自己的双手，仿佛托举着一条透明的哈达。看手相的人便说：男左女右。女孩把左手背在身后，把右手手掌对准湛蓝或是雾霾的天。

常常想世上可真有命运这种东西？它是物质还是精神？难道说我们的一生都早早地被一种符咒规定，谁都无力更改？我们的手难道真是螺纹唱盘，所有的祸福都像音符微缩其中？

当我沮丧的时候，当我彷徨的时候，当我孤独寂寞悲凉的时候，我便格外地相信命运，相信命运的不公平。

当我快乐的时候，当我幸福的时候，当我成功欣喜的时候，我格外地相信自己，相信只有耕耘才有收成。

渐渐地，我终于发现命运是我怯懦时的盾牌，当我叫嚷命运不公最响的时候，正是我预备逃遁的前奏。命运像一只筐，我把对自己的姑息、原谅以及所有的延宕都一股脑地塞进去，然后蒙一块宿命的挽纱。我背着它慢慢地向前走，心中滋生一种听天由命的漠然。

有时候也诧异自己的手。手心叶脉般的纹路还是那样琐细，但这只手做过的事情，却已有了几番变迁。

在喜马拉雅山、冈底斯山、喀喇昆仑山三山交会的高原上，我当过卫生员，用这只手推过注射器针管，扣动过冲锋枪的扳机。在机器轰鸣铜水飞溅的重工业厂区里，我做过主治医师和卫生所长，签过无数张处方，医治过数不清的病人。今天，当我用我的笔书写我对这个世界的想法时，我觉得是用我的手，把我的心制成薄薄的切片，置于人世沧桑的天平之上……

高原呼啸的风雪，卷走了我一生中最好的年华，并以浓重的阴影，投射于我此后行程中的每一处驿站。岁月送给我苦难，也附赠我经验与教训。我如今对命运的看法，与年少时有了巨大的改变。

当我快乐当我幸福当我成功当我优越当我欣喜的时候，当一切美好安稳莅临的时刻，我要提醒我自己——这是命运的环笼罩了我。在这个环里，居住着机遇，居住着偶然性，居住着所有帮助过我的人。

而当我遇到挫折和悲哀的时候，我便默不作声地走出那个怨天尤人的我，像孙悟空的分身术一样，跳起来，站在云头上，注视着那个不幸的人。于是，我清楚地看到了她的软弱，她的怯懦，她的虚荣以及她的愚昧……

年过花甲，我对命运已心平气和。

小时候是个女孩，大起来成为女人，总觉得做个女人要比男人难，大约以后成了老婆婆，也要比老爷爷累。生活中就像没有无缘无故的爱一样，也没有无缘无故的幸运。无端的幸运往往更像一场阴谋一个陷阱的开始。我不相信命运，我只相信我的手。

因为它不属于冥冥之中任何未知的力量，而只属于我的心。我可以支配它，去干我想干的任何一件事情。我不相信手掌的纹路，但我相信手掌加上手指所蕴积的力量。蓝天下的女孩，在你纤细的右手里，有一粒金苹果的种子。所有的人都看不见它，唯有你清楚地知道它将你的手心炙得发痛，那是你的梦想，你的期望。

女孩，握紧你的右手，千万别让它飞走！相信自己的手，相信它会在你的手里，长成棵会唱歌的金苹果树。

The Seed in Your Hand

A girl, arms outstretched and palms up as if holding out an invisible khata, can often be seen standing in front of a palm reader. After the palmist pronounces his usual "right hand for women and left hand for men," the girl, with her left hand put behind her now, will extend her right hand, with its palm facing the clear, blue sky or the mucky shroud of smog, as the case may be.

I often wonder if there is such a thing as fate at all. Is it tangible or spiritual? Are our lives all predestined, as if by an unshakable curse? Do creases in our palm conceal secret signs, like grooves of a gramophone record embedding harrowing notes, foreshadowing our fortune or fall?

When I felt crestfallen, lonely or lost, I tended to believe in fate and its unfairness more. When I revelled in success, I tended to have more faith in myself, believing that hard work would always pay.

I realized later that fate had often been an excuse for my cowardice. I begrudged the unfairness of fate most vocally when I was on the brink of throwing in the towel. It was a catchall pretext for self-forgiveness and lethargy. Fatalism then weighed on me as I trudged along in the daily grind with apathy and resignation.

Then I looked at my hands, amazed by the creases in the palms intricate like the veining of a leaf, which had accomplished so much through all the vicissitudes of my life.

As a medic of a highland army unit based at the junction of the three mighty mountain ranges — the Himalayas, Gangdise and Karakorum — I had used my hands to push the syringe needle and pull the trigger of my assault rifle. Then as an attending physician and clinic director in an industrial complex, I signed prescriptions that I had lost count of, healing the sick and saving many lives, in the midst of the constant clanking of heavy machinery, and droplets of molten metal arcing out of copper smelting furnaces. Now I use my pen to record my musings about the world, putting "thin slices" of my soul under microscopic examination, and sharing slivers of insight about life.

My stint on the Tibetan Plateau ate up most of my youthful years, like howling winds that sucked all the moisture out of highland air, casting long shadows on my life later. Those years of hardship had also given me precious lessons and experience, fundamentally changing my outlook on life.

I have learned that when I am content, happy, and blissful as if I were holding all the aces, I must remind myself that whatever success I have enjoyed is but a fortuitous convergence of opportunity and help from others. In moments of distress and sorrow, I should peel away quietly from my loathsome self, as if floating up and watching myself down below, like the Monkey King of the classic *Journey to the West* fame hovering in his avatar. Then, the detached I see my own frailty and cowardice, ignorance and unworthy conceit.

Now that I have turned sixty, rounding off the sexagenarian cycle, I have an innate sense of calm and acquiescence with fate.

In my youth and middle age, I always felt that, being female, I endured more hardship than the average man. Perhaps when I someday become a wobbly granny, I would fuss and dither more than a regular grandpa. I have always believed in working by the sweat of my brow, never holding out for any proverbial pie in the sky. Nothing comes of nothing; any unearned blessing is to me more like a dubious bad omen.

My able hands belong to me, not any unknown power. With them, I can accomplish anything that I set my mind to. I don't believe the foretelling of the lines in my palms, but rather the power of my hands and fingers. The girl that stands under the clear, blue sky in fact has in her delicate right hand a seed, unseen by all but herself. It is her aspiration and dream; glowing brightly and warm to the touch.

Hold on to the glowing seed in your hand and don't let it slip! Believe in the power of your own hands, with which you can bring your dream to fruition, from a tiny seed to a singing tree of golden apples.

风不能把阳光打败

　　"但是"这个连词，好似把皮坎肩缀在一起的丝线，多用在一句话的后半截，表示转折。

　　比方说：你这次的考试成绩不错，但是——强中自有强中手，你可不能骄傲啊。

　　比方说：这女孩身材不错，但是——皮肤黑了些，所以整体不能说是一个美女。

　　不知"但是"这个词刚发明的时候，对它前后意思的分量，切割得是否大致公允（也就是说，它只是一个单纯纽带，居中调停，并不偏谁向谁）。后来在长期的使用磨损中，分量就悄悄变了。无论在它之前，堆积了多少褒词，"但是"一出，便像撒了盐酸的污垢，优点就冒着泡沫没了踪影，只剩下残酷的结论。于是人们记住的总是贬义，好似爬上高坡，没来得及喘口匀气，"但是"一出手，不由分说就把你推下了谷底。

"但是"成了把人心捆成炸药包的细麻绳，成了马上有冷水泼面的前奏曲。它一露面，就让你把面前的温暖和光明淡忘，只留下遗憾懊恼。在"但是"的打击下，好样的会振起精神，迎击扑面而来的顿挫。孬的人，也许就一蹶不振了。

其实，所有的光明都有暗影，"但是"的本意，不过是强调事物立体。可惜日积月累的负面暗示，"但是"这个预报一出，就抹去了喜色，忽略了成绩，轻慢了进步，贬斥了攀升。

一位心理学家说，希望大家从此废弃"但是"，改用"同时"。

比如我们形容天气的时候，早先说："今天的太阳很好，但是风很大。"

今后说："今天的太阳很好，同时风很大。"

最初看这两句话的时候，好像没有多大差别。你不要急，轻声地多念几遍，那分量和语气的韵味，就体会出来了。

但是风很大——会把人的注意力聚焦在不利的因素上，觉着太阳好不是件值得高兴的事情，风大才是关键。借助了"但是"的威力，风把阳光打败。

Wind Cannot Blow Away Sunlight

The word "but" is often used as a conjunctive to indicate reversal or exception.

For example, people may say to you, "You did well in the exam, but there are others who did even better and you shouldn't be smug." Or "This girl is shapely but a little dark in complexion; not altogether beautiful."

I don't know if "but" has always been used to introduce such a negative tone or merely something in contrast. More often it seems to be the former. No matter how positive the statement before, but changes the tone, making the entire sentence altogether acetic and scathing, as if corrosive acid was poured over the lime scale. You are left with the impression of the derogatory that is demeaning to the dignity of endeavour. All efforts are rendered worthless by a blithe, dainty but.

But is the fuse of explosive anguish, signalling the advent of the chill — of having the carpet pulled from under your feet. It discourages you, wiping off any lingering warmth and brightness and leaving you with nothing but agony and regret. Only the truly brave will grit his teeth and fight on, whereas the lesser will not recover from the crushing blow of the mighty but.

It goes without saying that every light casts a shadow. But, as a conjunctive, should simply introduce something that contrasts what goes before it. However, with many habitually using it to link a negative statement, but often casts a shadow of negation, stifling the drive to accomplish, move forward, and soar.

A psychologist thus suggested using while instead of but.

For example, instead of saying "It's sunny but windy", we should say, "sunny while windy."

At first glance, the two statements may look quite alike. Well, repeat them a few more times and let them roll off your tongue ... You will notice the difference in tone and emphasis.

"But windy" focuses our attention on the unfavourable, as though the wind were the key and sunlight secondary. Wind obscures sunlight, with the mighty but.

心灵拒绝创可贴

我有过若干次讲演的经历，在北大和清华，在军营和监狱，在农村土坯搭建的课堂和美国最奢华的私立学校……面对从医学博士到纽约贫民窟的孩子等各色人群，我都会很直率地谈出对问题的想法。在我的记忆中，有一次的经历非常难忘。

那是一所很有名望的大学，约过我好几次了，说学生们期待和我进行讨论。我一直推辞，我从骨子里不喜欢演说。每逢答应一桩这样的公差，就要莫名地紧张好几天。但学校方面很执着，在第 N 次邀请的时候说：该校的学生思想之活跃甚至超过了北大，会对演讲者提出极为尖锐的问题，常常让人下不了台，有时演讲者简直是灰溜溜地离开学校。

听他们这样一讲，我的好奇心就被激励起来，我说，我愿意接受挑战。于是，我们就商定了一个日子。

那天，大学的礼堂挤得满满的，当我穿过密密的人群走向讲台的时候，心里涌起怪异的感觉，不知道今天将有怎样的场面出现。果然，从我一开始讲话，就不断地有条子递上来，不一会儿，就在手边积成了厚厚一堆，好像深秋时节被清洁工扫起的落叶。我一边演讲，一边充满了猜测，不知树叶中潜伏着怎样的思想炸弹。讲演告一段落，进入回答问题阶段，我迫不及待地打开了堆积如山的纸条，一张张阅读。那一瞬，台下变得死寂，偌大的礼堂仿若空无一人。

我看完了纸条说，有一些表扬我的话，我就不念了。除此之外，纸条上提得最多的问题是——"人生有什么意义？请你务必说真话，因为我们已经听过太多言不由衷的假话了"。

我念完这张纸条以后，台下响起了掌声。我说，你们今天提出这个问题很好，我会讲真话，我在西藏阿里的雪山之上，面对着浩瀚的苍穹和壁立的冰川，如同一个茹毛饮血的原始人，反复地思索过这个问题。我相信，一个人在他年轻的时候，是会无数次地叩问自己——我的一生，到底要追索怎样的意义？

我想了无数个晚上和白天，终于得到了一个答案。今天，在这里，我将非常负责地对大家说，我思索的结果是：人生是没有任何意义的！

这句话说完，全场出现了短暂的寂静，如同旷野。但是，紧接着就响起了暴风雨般的掌声。

那是我在讲演中获得的最热烈的掌声。在以前，我从来不相信有什么"暴风雨般的掌声"这种话，觉得那只是一个拙劣的比喻，但这一次，我相信了。我赶快用手做了一个"暂停"的手势，但掌声还是绵延了若干时间。

我说，大家先不要忙着给我鼓掌，我的话还没有说完。我说人生是没有意义的，这不错，但是——我们每一个人要为自己确立一个意义！

是的，关于人生的意义的讨论，充斥在我们周围。很多说法，由于熟悉和重复，已让我们从熟视无睹滑到了厌烦。可是，这不是问题的真谛。真谛是别人强加给你的意义，无论它多么正确，如果它不曾进入你的心理结构，它就永远是身外之物。比如我们从小就被家长灌输过人生意义的答案。在此后漫长的岁月里，谆谆告诫的老师和各种类型的教育，也都不断地向我们批发人生意义的补充版。但是，有多少人把这种外在的框架，当成了自己内在的标杆，并为之下定了奋斗终生的决心？

那一天结束讲演之后，我听到有同学说，他觉得最大的收获是听到有一个活生生的中年人亲口说，人生是没有意义的，你要为之确立一个意义。

其实，不单是中国的青年人在目标这个问题上飘忽不定，就是在美国的著名学府哈佛大学，也有很多人无法在青年时代就确立自己的目标。我看到一则材料，说某年哈佛的毕业生临出校门的时候，校方对他们做了一个有关人生目标的调查，结果是百分之二十七的人完全没有目标；百分之六十的人目标模糊；百分之十的人有近期目标；只有百分之三的人有着清晰而长远的目标。

二十五年过去了，那百分之三的人不懈地朝着一个目标坚忍努力，成了社会的精英，而其余的人成就要相差很多。

我之所以提到这个例子，是想说明在人生目标的确立上，无论中国还是外国的青年，都处于相当程度的朦胧或是混沌状态。有人会说，是啊，那又怎么样？我可以一边慢慢成长，一边寻找自己的人生意义啊。我平日也碰到很多的青年朋友，诉说他们的种种苦难。我在耐心地听完那些折磨他们的烦心事之后，把渴求的目光撒在一旁，我会问，你的人生目标是什么？

他们通常会很吃惊，好像怀疑我是否听懂了他们的愁苦，甚至恼怒我为什么对具体的问题视而不见，而盘问他们如此不着边际的空话。更有甚者，以为我根本就没有心思听他们说话，自己胡乱找了个话题来搪塞。

我会迎着他们疑虑的目光，说，请回答我的这个问题，你为什么而活着呢？

年轻人一般会很懊恼地说，这个问题太大了，和我现在遇到的事没有一点关联。我会说，你错了。世上的万事万物都有关联。有人常常以为心理上的事只和单一的外界刺激有关，就事论事，其实心理和人生的大目标有着纲举目张的紧密接触。很多心理问题，实际上都是人生的大目标出现了混乱和偏移。

举个例子。一个小伙子找到我，说他为自己说话很快而苦恼，他交了一个女朋友，感情很好。但女孩子不喜欢他说话太快。一听他口若悬河滔滔不绝地说个没完，女孩就说自己快变成大头娃娃了。还说如果他不改掉这毛病，就不能把他"引荐"给自己的妈妈，因为老人家最烦的就是说话爱吐唾沫星子的人。

您说我怎么才能改掉说话太快的毛病？他殷切地看着我，闹得我都觉得如果不帮他这个忙，简直就成了毁掉他一生爱情和事业的凶手。

我说，你为什么要讲话那么快呢？

他说，如果慢了，我怕人家没有耐心听完我的话。您知道，现在的社会，节奏那么快，你讲慢了，人家就跑了。

我说，如果按照你的这个观点发挥下去，社会节奏越来越快，你岂不是就得说绕口令了？你的准丈母娘就不是这样的人啊，她就喜欢说话速度慢一点并且注意礼仪的人啊。

他说，好吧，就算您说的这两种人都可以并存，但我还是觉得说话快一些，比较占便宜，可以在单位时间内传达更多的信息。

我说，那你的关键就是期待别人能准确地接受你的信息。你以为只有快速发射信息才是唯一的途径。你对自己的观点并不自信。

他说，正是这样。我生怕别人不听我的，我就快快地说，多多地说。当他这样说完之后，连自己也笑起来。我说，其实别人能否接受我们的观点，语速并不是最重要的。而且，你能告诉我，你为什么这样在意别人是否能接受你的观点？

这个说话很快的男孩突然语塞起来，忸怩着说，我把理想告诉你，你可不要笑话我。

我连连保证绝不泄密。他说，我的理想是当一个政治家。所有的政治家都很雄辩，您说对吧？

我说，这咱们就比较接触到问题的实质了。要当一个政治家，第一要自信。他们的雄辩不是来自速度，而是来自信念。一个自信的人，不论说话快还是慢，他们对自我信念的坚守流露出来，会感染他人。我知道你有如此远大的理想，这很好。你要做的事，不是把话越说越快，而是积攒自己的力量，让自己的信念更加坚强。

那一天的谈话就到此为止。后来，这个男生告诉我，他讲话的速度就慢了下来，也被"批准"见到了自己的准丈母娘，听说很受欢迎。

这边刚刚解决了一个说话快的问题，紧接着又来了一位女硕士，说自己的心理问题是讲话太慢，周围的人都认为她有很深的城府，不敢和她交朋友，以为在她那些缓慢吐出的话语背后，隐藏着怎样的阴谋。

我试了很多方法，却无法让自己说话快起来，烦死了。她慢吞吞地对我这样说，语速的确有一种压抑人的迟缓，好像在话的背后还隐藏着另一句话。

我看她急迫的神情，知道她非常焦虑。

我说，你讲每一句话是否都要经过慎重的考虑？

她说，是啊。如果不考虑，讲错了话，谁负得了这个责？

我说，你为什么特别怕讲错话？

女硕士说，因为我输不起。我家庭背景不好，家里有人犯了罪，周围的人都看不起我；家里很穷，从小靠亲戚的施舍我才能坚持学业。我生怕一句话说差了，人家不高兴，就不给我学费了。所以，连问一句"你吃了吗"这样中国人最普通的话，我也要三思而后行。我怕人家说"你连自己的饭都吃不饱，也配来问别人吃饭问题"。

听到这里，我说我明白了。你觉得自己的每一句话都可能引致他人的误解，给自己造成不良影响。

女硕士连连说，对对，就是这样的。

我笑了，说，你这一句话说得并不慢啊。

她说，那我是相信你不会误会我。

我说，这就对了。你说话速度慢，不是一个技术性的问题，是你不能相信别人。你是否准备一辈子都不相信任何人？如果是这样的话，我断定你的讲话速度是不会改变的。如果你从此相信他人，讲话的速度自然会比较适宜，既不会太慢，也不会太快，而是能收放自如。

那个女生后来果然有了很大的改变，她的人际关系也有了进步。

今天我们从一个很大的目标谈起，结果要在一个很小的地方结束。我想说，一个人的心理是一座斗拱飞檐的宫殿，这座宫殿的基础就是我们对自己人生目标的规划和对世界、对他人的基本看法。一些看起来是技术和表面的问题，其实内里都和我们的基本人生观有着千丝万缕的联系。心理问题切不可头痛医头、脚痛医脚，那样如同创可贴，只能暂时封住小伤口，却无法从根本上让我们的精神强健起来。

No Band-aid for Our Soul

I have had some experience in public speaking — at Peking and Tsinghua Universities, in army barracks and prisons, in village classrooms with rammed-earth walls and elite private schools in the US ... My audience ranged from M.D. candidates to children from the slums of New York City. I always spoke my mind when addressing questions put to me.

There is one talk that stands out in my memory. It was at a prestigious university. I had declined their invitation several times before, despite the plea that their students were eager to have a dialogue with me. Public speaking was never my strong suit. I tended to get inexplicably nervous days before any such event.

However, the university was persistent, saying that their students were intellectually rigorous, more so than even those at Peking University, and sometimes their tough questions would put the speaker on the spot and even send some trotting off in a huff.

My curiosity was piqued. I decided to accept the challenge, and a date was confirmed.

The auditorium was packed on the day. I wondered what was in store for me that day. Sure enough, the moment I began, slips of paper with questions scribbled on them kept arriving and soon formed a pile, like collected leaves of a hundred autumn hues. As I talked, my thoughts strayed to the pile, wondering what bombshell questions could be hidden there. As I concluded my talk, I hastened to open the slips of paper and read the questions one after another. The cavernous hall fell completely silent as though it were deserted.

Apart from praises which I put aside, the

questions showed up most were, "What is the meaning of life?" with one beseeching me to "Speak the truth, for we are sick of oblique answers!"

After I read that note aloud, the audience applauded. I said, "This is a good question and I will speak the truth. When I was in Ngari, Tibet, facing the snow-capped mountains and perpendicular glaciers, becoming almost a primitive nomad myself, I had often thought of the same question. I believe that, when young, one will indeed often ask oneself, 'What is the meaning of my struggle in this life?' Day and night I had contemplated the question and I finally found the answer. Today, I will share with you my answer in all seriousness: There is no meaning to life!"

There was a moment of stunned silence. Then a thunderous applause broke out. It was the most roaring applause I had ever received. I had always brushed off expressions like "thunderous applause" as clumsy exaggerations. But on that occasion, it was in fact true. I hastened to raise a hand for silence, but the applause continued for a while before tapering off.

I said, "You shouldn't have rushed to applaud me. I haven't finished. I said that life has no meaning. It's up to each of us to confer meaning on our own lives!"

It is true that there has been so much talk about the meaning of life. Some views are but repetitions of others, which are tiresome and off-putting. But that is not the point. The point is any meaning imposed on us, no matter how proper, will remain foreign if it is not internalized as part of our psyche. Since childhood, we have been fed various versions of "meaning of life" by our parents, teachers and instructors of all descriptions. Yet how many of us have internalized those imposed notions and found the purpose in our lives?

After the talk, a student told me that the greatest lesson for him that day was hearing a person halfway through her life saying life had no meaning, and everyone had to find the meaning for themselves.

I once came across a Harvard report: when questioned upon commencement about their goals in life, 27% of the graduates had no plans at all, 60% were vague, 10% had short-term plans, and only 3% had clear, long-term plans for their future. Twenty-five years later, the 3% became social elites while the rest had done poorly in comparison.

I cite this report to point out that both in China and around the world, the young tend to be vague and oblivious when it comes to their plans for the future. They may say — "So what?" They are still growing and will take their time to find their own version of the meaning of life. I have also heard from many young people their gripes about life being tough. After patiently hearing them out, I would turn away from their expectant looks and ask, "What are your goals in life?"

Often, they were stumped, suspecting if I had misunderstood or was ignoring their complaints, and was bugging them with frivolous rhetoric. Some even suspected I had no interest at all in their problems and had thrown at them a random and irrelevant question. I would look them in the eye and demand, "Please answer my question. What are you living for?"

Most would fret, "It is such a broad question and irrelevant to our immediate problems." To that I would say, "You are wrong." Everything in the world is interconnected. Some assume that their psychological problem has to do with a single, external shock and treat it as such. As a matter of fact, one's psychological constitution has much to do with one's overall goal in life. Many psychological problems arise from confusion and deviation regarding one's purpose in life.

A case in point: a young man once came to me with a problem — he talked too fast. He had found a girlfriend and they liked each other. But the girl was bothered by his talking too fast. The torrent of words he poured out would make her head swim. She said if he didn't get rid of this bad habit, she could not take him home to meet her parents, for her mother detested people babbling with flecks of spit flying about.

"So how can I get rid of this troubling habit?" he asked with a pleading look, as if I would be held accountable for wrecking his marriage and career prospects, should I refuse to help.

"Why do you need to talk so fast?" I asked.

"If I slow down, I fear people will lose patience," said he. "You know how it is nowadays — the pace of life being so fast!"

"Well, following your line of thinking, as the society moves faster and faster, you would have to talk in the manner of speaking tongue twisters. Your prospective mother-in-law apparently doesn't think so, by your own account. She seems to prefer speech to be measured, with some regard to manners, too."

"Okay," he conceded. "But I still prefer talking fast, even if both ways of speaking are acceptable. You have the advantage of getting more information across within the given timeframe."

"In which case," I said, "the key is that your views can be correctly understood and accepted by others. Do you think you can achieve that by firing off messages as quickly as possible? This to me suggests a lack of confidence more than anything else."

"That's true," he conceded again. "I worry people would reject me, so I talk fast to squeeze in as much as possible." He chuckled, laughing at himself.

"Actually," I pointed out, "whether others accept or reject our views does not depend on how fast we talk. Besides, why should you worry so much whether others accept your views or not?" The young man was flummoxed, saying coyly, "I will tell you the reason if you promise not to laugh at me." I consented. "I want to become a politician. All politicians are orators, aren't they?" offered the young man.

"Now we know the crux of the matter — you want to go into politics. In that case, for starters, you must have self-confidence. A politician's eloquence does not come from speed, but confidence. He inspires his audiences by the strength of his convictions, whether he speaks fast or slowly. It is good that you have such an ideal. But what you need is not talking faster and faster. You should strengthen your convictions."

Thus we ended our conversation. Later, the young man told me that his speech had slowed down and that he did meet and was warmly welcomed by his prospective mother-in-law.

Just as I had dealt with the young man who talked too fast, a graduate student came with her problem of talking too slowly. People kept away, she said, suspecting unseemly secrecy because of the hesitant, unforthcoming way she talked.

"I had tried, but I just couldn't make myself speak faster. It is so annoying," she said languidly. Her halting voice did carry with it a sense of depression, as if each word she uttered had another meaning hidden underneath.

I felt the urgency in her plea and could see she was depressed.

"Do you always weigh your words when you speak?" asked I.

"Of course," she said. "If you utter a wrong word, who is

going to be responsible but you yourself?"

"But why are you so afraid of saying the wrong thing?" I pursued.

"I can't afford to make a mistake. My family background is not so good. A family member ran afoul of the law, so we are despised in the neighbourhood. Besides, we are not well off. I had to depend on the support from relatives for my schooling since childhood. I am afraid of speaking out of turn, offending the relatives and losing their support. I even hesitate to use the most common Chinese greeting 'Have you eaten?' People might say, 'You can't even feed yourself. What's the point of asking if we have eaten?'"

Now I understand, I said. "You fear that every word you say might be misinterpreted and used against you?"

"That's it!" she concurred immediately.

"Now, that was a quick answer," said I, laughing.

"That's because I believe that you will not misunderstand."

"That's right. Your slow speech is not a physiological problem. It's because you can't trust others. Are you going to spend your whole life distrusting people around you? If yes, I am certain your speech speed will never pick up. If you begin to trust people more, it will become normal and natural, neither too slow nor too fast."

Later, the girl did improve her speech, as well as her relationship with others.

That day, I concluded my talk by saying: "Today we started out on a big topic, and will end in a very small place. I want to say that a person's psychology is like a castle with flying eaves. The foundation for this castle is his plan for life, as well as his view of other people and the world at large. Some problems that appear at first glance to be technical are in fact inextricably linked to our worldview. Psychological problems cannot be dealt with by focusing only on the superficial signs. That would be like applying a band-aid for a small wound — it won't help in the fundamentals, which is to boost our spirit that makes us strong."

致不美丽的女孩子

有一天，我收到了一封读者来信，撕开之后，落下来一张照片。先看了照片，没什么特别的感觉，待看了信件之后，心脏的部位就有些酸胀的感觉。我赶快伏案，写了一封回信（是手写的，不是用电脑打出来的。我在回信这件事上，坚持手工操作）。

现在征得那位女孩子的同意，把她的信和我的回复一并登出来，但愿她的父母会看到。

毕阿姨:

　　您好!

　　我有一个痛入心肺的问题。我的爸爸妈妈都长得很好看,简直就是美女和帅哥的超级组合(他们那个年代还没有这样时髦的词,好像用的是"秀丽"和"精干"这两个形容词)。人们都以为他们会生出一个金童玉女来,可惜我就恰恰取了他们的缺点组合在一起了,长得一点儿也不漂亮。我从小就习惯了人们见到我时的惊讶——哟,这个小姑娘长得怎么一点儿也不像她的爸爸妈妈啊!最令人伤感的是,我爸爸妈妈也经常会这么说,同时面露极度的失望之色。为此,我非常难过,也不愿和他们在一起走。现在唯一的希望就是他们快快老起来,那时候,他们就不会太好看了,而我还年轻,是不是可以弥补一下先天的不足啊?您说呢?寄上一张我的照片,但愿不会吓着您。

肖晓

肖晓:

　　你好!

　　我看到了你寄来的照片,情况不像你说的那样悲惨啊!相片上,你是一个很可爱很阳光的少女哦!也许你的父母真是美男子和美女的超级组合(遗憾你没有寄来一张合影,那样的话,我也可以养养盯着电脑太久而昏花的双眼了），在这样的父母笼罩之下，真是很容易生出自卑的感觉，此乃人之常情，你不必觉得这是自己的错。不过，如果你的父母也这样埋怨你，你尽可以据理力争。找一个至爱亲朋大聚会的场合，隆重地走到众人面前，一本正经地说，嘿，大家请注意，我是一件产品，内在的质量还是很好的，至于外表，那是把我制造出来的设计师的事，你们如果有意见，就找他们去提吧，或者把产品退回去要求返修，把外观再打磨一下。但愿当你说完这番话之后，大家会面面相觑，微笑着不再说什么了。

人们总是非常愿意评价他人的长相，有时单凭长相就在第一时间做出若干判断。这也许是从远古时代就流传下来的一种近乎本能的习惯，那时候的人会凭借着长相判断对方和自己是不是同属于一个部落和宗族，是不是有良好的营养和体力，甚至性情和脾气也能从面部皱纹的走向看出端倪来。现代人有了很多进步，但在以貌取人这方面，基本上还在沿用旧例，改变不大。有一句流传很广的话是这样说的——人的长相这件事，在三十五岁之前是要父母负责的，但在三十五岁之后就要自己负责了。我有时在公园看到面目慈祥很有定力的老女人，心中就会充满了感动。要怎样的风霜才能勾勒出这样的线条和风采，我们看到的不再是先天的美貌桑叶，它们已经被岁月之蚕噬咬得只剩下筋络，华贵属于天地的精华和不断蜕皮的修炼。

从相片上看你还很年轻，长相的公案，目前就推给你的父母吧。我希望你健康地长大，但中年以后的事恐怕就要你自己负责了。如果你实在不想再听这些议论了，唯一的办法是找到一卷无边无际的胶带，牢牢地封住他们的嘴巴。看到这里，我猜你会说，你开的这个方子好是好，可我现在到哪里去找那卷无边无际的胶带呢？就是找到了，我能不能买得起？

这卷胶带在哪里，我也不知道。它是怎样的价钱，我也不知道。找找看吧，到网上搜索一番，请大家一齐帮忙找。如果实在是上穷碧落下黄泉也找不到，就只有最后一个法子，那就是让人们说去吧，你可以我行我素，依然快乐和努力地干自己想干的事。

Letter to a Plain-looking Girl

One day I received a letter from a reader. As I slit open the envelope, a photo slipped out. I took a glance and found nothing unusual. Then I unfurled the letter and felt a momentary twinge inside after I had read it. I dashed out a reply (not on my computer. I insist on writing replies to my readers by hand.)

Now, with consent from the girl, here are her letter and my reply, both of which I hope her parents may have a chance to read.

Dear Ms. Bi,

Greetings!

I have a problem that has gnawed at my heart. Both my parents are good-looking, a dream couple, so to speak (though back in their time they didn't have such a fancy description and might simply have been called pretty and handsome). Everybody thought their offspring would be good-looking, too. However, I didn't take after them at all, and have instead picked up all their imperfections. In childhood, I had grown used to other people's shocked reaction when they saw me resembling neither of my parents. What hurt me most was my parents, too, often saying the same thing, hardly hiding their disappointment. Because of this, I feel sad and don't even want to be seen walking by their side. My only hope now is that they age quickly. Then, they won't look as gorgeous as they are now while I will still be young, which will make up for my plain looks. Wouldn't you agree?

Enclosed please find a photo of mine. Hope it won't give you goose bumps.

Yours sincerely,

Xiao Xiao

Dear Xiao Xiao,

Thank you for your letter. I have seen your photo and, contrary to your self-description, what I saw is a lovely, cheerful girl! Perhaps your parents are a dream couple—pretty wife and handsome husband (pity that you didn't enclose a photo of theirs, too; might very well be candy for my eyes that are strained after staring at the computer for too long). True, living in the shadow of good-looking parents, one may be prone to feeling inferior. Though such a feeling is natural, your looks are not your fault. Should your parents blame you, you could certainly argue in your own defence. Pick a time when family relatives or friends gather and present yourself solemnly, "Hi, everyone! Let me introduce myself. I am a product of good quality on the inside. As for my looks—the packaging, they are its designers' masterwork. If you don't like the look of it, please raise it with them, or even ask for polishing or rework." It is my hope that they would chuckle and then shut up, after exchanging some uncomfortable looks.

People are keen to appraise others' looks and make judgement based on appearances. You may call it a custom, or instinct, with roots in humanity's ancient past, when ascertaining friend or foe by appearances and tribal features was crucial to survival. Even a person's state of nutrition, physical strength and temperament could be told by their facial wrinkles and furrows. We have come a long way. However, in judging people by their looks, we are not that different from our forebears of old.

There is a popular belief that one's looks are of one's own making beyond the age of thirty-five. Before that, you have your parents to blame. The sight of a kindly, calm old woman in the park always moved me deeply during my occasional walks there. What tribulations of life could have etched such grooves in her face and given her such aplomb. Time, like the silkworm, had eaten away the tender green of her prime, leaving lines of parched veining. The elegance of the elderly lady comes from heavenly endowment and trials and strife in her life.

I can see from the photo that you are still in your salad years and surely you have your parents to blame for your looks for now. I hope you grow up healthy and by the time you leave your adolescence behind, you will then be responsible for how you look. If you are tired of all the petty chattering, I can imagine your wishing for some magical tape that could seal up their mouths for good. And I imagined you might fret if you could ever have such a magical thing or if you had the money to pay for it.

I have no clue as to where to find such a tape and how much the seller would want to fetch. Maybe you can resort to the all-knowing internet and crowd-source? If in the end it is still nowhere to be found, then you will have to simply ignore them. Let them chatter all they want; get on with your life, do what you enjoy doing and brilliantly smile.

79

看着别人的眼睛

很小的时候，如果我有了过失，说了谎话，又不愿承认的时候，妈妈就会说：看着我的眼睛。如果我襟怀坦荡，我就敢看着她的眼睛，否则就只有羞愧地低头。

从此，我面对别人的时候，看着他的眼睛。

当我失败的时候，看着亲人的眼睛，我无地自容。但悲伤会使我的眼睛噙满泪水，却不会使我闭上眼睛。看着批评我的目光，我会激起正视缺点的勇气与信念。我会仔细回顾我走过的路，看看自己是怎样跌倒的，今后避开同样的危险。

当我得到表扬的时候，我也快乐地注视着别人的眼睛。我不喜欢假装谦虚把睫毛深深地垂下，一个人回到僻静处悄悄地乐。我愿意把心中的喜悦像满桶的水一样溢出来，让我的朋友们分享。在我的亲人、我的朋友的眼睛里，我读出他们的快活和对我更高的希冀。表扬不仅没有使我忘乎所以，反倒使我感到肩上的担子更加沉重。成功好比是一座小山，一个准备走很远的路的旅人，站得高了，才会看到目的地的篝火。他会加快自己的脚步。

当我面对陌生人的时候，我会格外注视他的眼睛。眼睛是心灵的窗户，这已经是被说腻了的古话，可我要说眼睛不仅仅是窗户，它还是心灵的家。假如陌生人的目光坦诚而友好，我会向他伸出我的手。假如陌生人的目光犹疑而彷徨，我断定他是一个没有主见的人，不能与他成为朋友。假如陌生人的目光躲闪而阴暗，我会退避三舍，在心里敲起警钟。假如陌生人的目光孤苦无告，我愿意提供力所能及的帮助。

当我面对熟识的人的时候，我会观察他的眼睛有没有变化。岁月会改变一个人的眼光，就像油漆的家具会变色一样。但是有些老朋友的眼光是不会变的，像最清澈的水晶，晶莹一生。但他们的眼睛会随着喜怒哀乐变换颜色，作为朋友，我愿与他们分担。假如他们悲哀，我愿为他们宽心。假如他们喜悦，我愿与他们分享。假如他们焦虑，我愿出谋划策。假如他们忧郁，我愿陪着他们沿着静静的小河走很远很远。

当我独自一人面对镜子的时候，我严格地审视自己的眼睛。它是否还保持着童年人的纯真与善良？它是否还凝聚着少年人的敏锐与蓬勃？它在历尽沧桑以后，是否还向往人世间的真善美？面对今后岁月的风霜雨雪，它是否依旧满怀勇气与希望？

当我面对森林的时候，我注视着森林的眼睛。它们就是树干上斑驳的年轮和随风摇曳的无数嫩叶。它们既苍老又年轻，流露出大自然无限的生机。

当我在月夜里面对星空的时候，我注视着宇宙的眼睛。那是苍穹无数的星辰。天是那样幽蓝而辽阔，周围是那样静寂而悠远。作为一个单独的人，我们是多么渺小啊！但正是看似微不足道的人类，开始了征服宇宙的长征。在这个意义上，人类又是那样伟大而悲壮。每一个孤立的人，都像小星星一样微弱，但集结起来，就可以给迷途的人指引方向，就可以在黑暗中放出光明。

我注视着滔滔的流水，浪花就是它的眼睛。生命在于运动，假如大海没有了波涛，就结束了它浩瀚博大的使命，大海就瞎了，成为死水一潭，再也不能负载舟楫远航，再也不能任海鸥翱翔，再也不能繁养无数的水族，再也不能驮着我们在海滩上嬉戏……

世界上所有的生灵都有它们的眼睛，就看你用不用心寻找，就看你有没有勇气和它对视。

当我刚刚开始学习注视别人的眼睛的时候，心中很有些不安。我觉得自己是个小小的孩童，我怎么敢看着别人的眼睛？那不是太不尊敬人了吗？我对妈妈讲了我的顾虑。她笑了，说，那你明天试着看看老师的眼睛。

第二天，在课堂上，我开始注视着老师的眼睛。好怪啊，老师好像专门给我一个人讲课似的。我的思考紧紧地跟随老师的讲解，在知识的密林里寻觅。当讲到重要的地方，我看到老师的眼睛里冒出精彩的火花，我知道自己一定要记住它。当老师的眼光像湖水一样平静的时候，我知道这只需要一般掌握。当我在读老师的眼睛的时候，老师也在读我的眼睛。假如我显现出迷惘与困惑，老师就会停顿他讲解的步伐，在原地连兜几个圈子，直到我的目光重又明亮如洗。假如我调皮地向他眨眨眼睛，他会突然把讲了一半的话咽进嘴里。他知道我已心领神会，可以继续向下讲了。

我这才知道，眼睛对眼睛，是可以说话的。它们进行无声的交流，在这种通行的世界语里，容不得谎言，用不着翻译。它们比嘴巴更真实地反映出一个人隐秘的内心世界。

随着年龄的增长，我明白了注视着别人的眼睛是一种郑重，是一种尊敬，是一种信任，是一种坦诚。

当然了，这种注视不是死瞪瞪地盯着人家看，那样可真有点儿傻乎乎并且不文雅了。注视的目光应该是宁静而安然的，好像是我们在晴朗的天气眺望远处的青山。

如果我听懂了他的话，我会轻轻地点头。如果我需要他详细解说，我会用目光传达出这种请求。

注视着别人的眼睛，也给自己提出了更高的要求。

当我注视着别人的眼睛说"谢谢你"的时候，我必须发自内心地真诚。

当我注视着别人的眼睛说"对不起"的时候，我必须传递由衷的歉意。

当我注视着别人的眼睛说"我能把这件事做好"时，我一定要有"下一个必胜"的信心。

当我注视着别人的眼睛说"请相信我"时，我觉得自己陡然间增长了才干和胆魄。

医学家证明，人在说谎的时候，无论他多么历练老辣，他的眼睛都会泄露他的秘密。他的瞳孔会扩散变大，他的视线会游移，眼睑也会不由自主地下垂。

为了我们能够勇敢地注视别人的眼睛并且不怕被别人注视，让我们做一个襟怀坦荡、心灵像水晶般透明的人。

Look Me in the Eye

When I was little, whenever I had done something wrong and refused to admit it, or had lied, my mother would say, "Look me in the eye." I would hang my head in shame, for I'd only dare to look into her eyes if I had nothing to hide.

I had since learned to look at other people's eyes when meeting them.

I looked into the eyes of the loved ones when I had let them down, with a pang of remorse and repentance. In anguish and sorrow, my eyes would be large and brimming with tears. Looking those critical of me in the eye, I was thus emboldened to examine the path I had taken, how I had stumbled and how to avoid similar perils in future.

When others praised me, I meet their eyes with joy, not feigning humility with a shy, downcast stare. I share my joy with friends, letting it overflow, rather than relishing it by myself. Staring into the eyes of my loved ones and friends, I read their joy, as well as their expectations for me to do even better. Their praises make me keenly aware of the weight of duty. Success is like gaining the top of a hill, one of many on a long trek, where you see the campfire at the day's end. It urges you to hasten.

When I meet someone for the first time, I pay special attention to their eyes. If "eyes are the window to the soul," very much a cliché now, they are also its home. If I see candour and friendliness in the eyes of a stranger, I extend my hand. If I see hesitation and uncertainty, I know he is indecisive and not a person to befriend. If I see evasiveness and glum, I will be alarmed and back off. If I see sorrow and helplessness, I will help in any way I can.

When I see an acquaintance, I look at his eyes for any

sign of change. Time changes many things — a man's gaze, the fading paint of a heirloom cabinet. Yet with some old friends, I see in their eyes unchanging clarity and glint, like the purest crystal. They tell me their joy, fury and sorrow. I share their delight, comfort them in their moments of anguish, counsel them when they are tormented by anxiety, and quietly walk with them along the river when they are glum.

When I am alone, I look at my eyes in the mirror, examining them intently, to see if they have kept the innocence and goodness of the child and the zestful sharpness of youth. Do they still yearn for truth, beauty and goodness after all the tribulations in my life? Are they still full of hope and courage?

When I see a forest, I look at its eyes, too — the markings in the trunk and the shimmering leaves of the trees, ancient yet tender, showing nature's boundless power and life.

When I gaze at the starry sky, I see eyes of the heaven — stars in their multitudes. Under the unfathomable vastness, depth, and in timeless silence, an individual is infinitely small. Yet humanity, insignificant on the cosmic scale, has the boldness to explore the deep space, which is nothing short of heroic. Humans are like stars in the night sky, each twinkling and tiny, yet together forming constellations that give direction to the wayfarer and meaning to chaos.

When I look at surging waves, the breakers are their eyes, too. Oceans are alive with the ebbs and flows of tides. Without the oceans in constant motion, there would have been no life — no ocean-going vessels, no soaring seagulls, no marine organisms in their astounding diversity, and no families playing on the beaches ... All creatures on earth have eyes. It takes patience to find, and courage to look into, them.

When I first stared into others' eyes, I felt a great unease. Being a small child, I felt daunted to look others in the eye. Would I be too disrespectful? I told mom my fears. She laughed, saying I should try looking my teacher in the eye.

So, in my classroom next day, I stared at my teacher's eyes. How strange! I felt as though he was talking to me alone. My mind followed his words keenly, as though I were wandering in an enchanted wood. I saw the glint in the teacher's eyes as he drove home a point that I should remember well. Then I saw placidness in his eyes; I knew he was touching on some general points. As I tried to read my teacher's eyes, the reverse was happening, too. If he sensed confusion and bewilderment, he would pause and regress until he saw my eyes shine and become clear again. Should I wink impishly, he would swallow his words mid-sentence, for he knew I had already gotten the point and he should simply skip and move ahead.

It dawned on me that eyes could communicate without words. They speak a universal language —

of a sort that neither tolerates lying nor needs interpretation. They reveal, more truthfully than the mouth, the inner world of an individual.

As I grew older, I learned that to look others in the eye is to treat them with respect, trust, sincerity and honesty.

Of course, staring into someone's eyes fixedly and unrelentingly can be daft and unabashed. Our gaze should be relaxed and serene, as though looking upon distant, verdant hills on a fine day.

I nod gently if I understood someone's intent in his eyes. If I need his elaboration, I show it with a beseeching look in my eye.

When I look others in the eye, I subject myself to a higher standard. When I thank someone while looking him in the eye, I must be sincere in my appreciation. When I apologize, my eyes convey true repentance. When I promise someone while looking him in eye, I must be convinced that I will not fail him. When I ask someone to trust me while looking him in the eye, I feel I am indeed in possession of great courage and prowess.

Medical research has shown that when a person is telling a lie, his eyes give him away, no matter how beguiling he may be. The pupils of his eyes dilute; he breaks eye contact; his eyelids involuntarily droop.

Let us be honest, sincere and openhearted, so that we are unafraid of holding eye contact, brave in our gaze, and our heart transparent as crystal.

我很重要

当我说出"我很重要"这句话的时候，颈项后面掠过一阵战栗。我知道这是把自己的额头裸露在弓箭之下了，心灵极容易被别人的批判洞伤。许多年来，没有人敢在光天化日之下表示自己"很重要"。我们从小受到的教育都是——"我不重要"。

作为一名普通士兵，与辉煌的胜利相比，我不重要。

作为一个单薄的个体，与浑厚的集体相比，我不重要。

作为一位奉献型的女性，与整个家庭相比，我不重要。

作为随处可见的人的一分子，与宝贵的物质相比，我们不重要。

我们——简明扼要地说，就是每一个单独的"我"——到底重要还是不重要？

我是由无数星辰日月草木山川的精华汇聚而成的。只要计算一下我们一生吃进去多少谷物，饮下了多少清水，才凝聚成一具生气蓬勃的躯体，我们一定会为那数字的庞大而惊讶。平日里，我们尚要珍惜一粒米、一叶菜，难道可以对亿万粒菽粟亿万滴甘露濡养出的万物之灵，掉以丝毫的轻心吗？

当我在博物馆里看到北京猿人窄小的额和前凸的吻时，我为人类原始时期的粗糙而黯然。他们精心打制出的石器，用今天的目光来看不过是极简单的玩具。如今幼小的孩童，就能熟练地操纵语言，我们才意识到已经在进化之路上前进了多远。我们的头颅就是一部历史，无数祖先进步的痕迹储存于脑海深处。我们是一株亿万年苍老树干上最新萌发的绿叶，不单属于自身，更属于土地。人类的精神之火，是连绵不断的链条，作为精致的一环，我们否认了自身的重要，就是推卸了一种神圣的承诺。

回溯我们诞生的过程，两组生命基因的嵌合，更是充满了人所不能把握的偶然性。我们每一个个体，都是机遇的产物。

一种令人怅然以至走入恐惧的想象，像雾霭一般不可避免地缓缓升起，模糊了我们的来路和去处，令人不得不断然打住思绪。

我们的生命，端坐于概率垒就的金字塔的顶端。面对大自然的鬼斧神工，我们还有权利和资格说我不重要吗？

对于我们的父母，我们永远是不可重复的孤本。无论他们有多少儿女，我们都是独特的一个。

假如我不存在了，他们就空留一份慈爱，在风中蛛丝般飘荡。

假如我生了病，他们的心就会皱缩成石块，无数次向上苍祈祷我的康复，甚至愿灾痛以十倍的烈度降临于他们自身，以换取我的平安。

我的每一滴成功，都如同经过放大镜，进入他们的瞳孔，摄入他们心底。

假如我们先他们而去，他们的白发会从日出垂到日暮，他们的泪水会使太平洋为之涨潮。面对这无法承载的亲情，我们还敢说我不重要吗？

我们的记忆，同自己的伴侣紧密地缠绕在一处，像两种混淆于一碟的颜色，已无法分开。你原先是黄，我原先是蓝，我们共同的颜色是绿，绿得生机勃勃，绿得苍翠欲滴。失去了妻子的男人，胸口就缺少了生死攸关的肋骨，心房裸露着，随着每一阵轻风滴血。失去了丈夫的女人，就是齐斩斩折断的琴弦，每一根都在雨夜长久地自鸣……面对相濡以沫的同道，我们忍心说我不重要吗？

俯对我们的孩童，我们是至高至尊的唯一。我们是他们最初的宇宙，我们是深不可测的海洋。假如我们隐去，孩子就永失淳厚无双的血缘之爱，天倾东南，地陷西北，万劫不复。盘子破裂可以粘起，童年碎了，永不复原。伤口流血了，没有母亲的手为他包扎。面临抉择，没有父亲的智慧为他谋略……面对后代，我们有胆量说我不重要吗？

与朋友相处，多年的相知，使我们仅凭一个微蹙的眉尖、一次睫毛的抖动，就可以明了对方的心情。假如我不在了，就像计算机丢失了一份不曾复制的文件，他的记忆库里留下不可填补的黑洞。夜深人静时，手指在揿了几个电话键码后，骤然停住，那一串数字再也用不着默诵了。逢年过节时，她写下一沓沓的贺卡。轮到我的地址时，她闭上眼睛……许久之后，她将一张没有地址只有姓名的贺卡填好，在无人的风口将它焚化。

相交多年的密友，就如同沙漠中的古陶，摔碎一件就少一件，再也找不到一模一样的成品。面对这般友情，我们还好意思说我不重要吗？

我很重要。

我对于我的工作我的事业，是不可或缺的主宰。我的独出心裁的创意，像鸽群一般在天空翱翔，只有我才捉得住它们的羽毛。我的设想像珍珠一般散落在海滩上，等待着我把它用金线串起。我的意志向前延伸，直到地平线消失的远方……没有人能替代我，就像我不能替代别人。我很重要。

我对自己小声说，我还不习惯嘹亮地宣布这一主张，我们在不重要中生活得太久了。我很重要。

我重复了一遍。声音放大了一点。我听到自己的心脏在这种呼唤中猛烈地跳动。我很重要。

我终于大声地对世界这样宣布。片刻之后，我听到山岳和江海传来回声。

是的，我很重要。我们每一个人都应该有勇气这样说。我们的地位可能很卑微，我们的身份可能很渺小，但这丝毫不意味着我们不重要。

重要并不是伟大的同义词，它是心灵对生命的允诺。

人们常常从成就事业的角度，断定我们是否重要。但我要说，只要我们在时刻努力着，为光明在奋斗着，我们就是无比重要地生活着。

让我们昂起头，对着我们这颗美丽的星球上的无数生灵，响亮地宣布——

我很重要。

I Am Important

"I am important!" Hardly are these words out when I felt a shiver down my spine. I have stuck my neck out and made myself an easy target of others' censure. Few ever dared to declare in broad daylight his or her self-importance. We have all been taught since we were little: "I am not important."

As a foot soldier, I don't matter in the grand scheme of things — the grand victory.

As a feeble individual, I am secondary to the collective.

As a dedicated wife and mother, family always comes first.

As a member of the ubiquitous, overflowing humanity, I am of little value in light of the scarcity of material resources.

It begs the question — if we, consisting of countless I's, are of any importance at all.

As a human being, I am a perfect specimen — epitome of essential elements of Mother Earth, with its majestic mountains and winding rivers, and forces of the cosmos. To sustain our divinely made body, we are shocked to learn, we consume such vast amounts of grain and water over a lifetime. We have been taught to cherish every grain of rice and every leaf of green, how can we belittle ourselves, a universe in a human body made of billions of grains and water molecules?

When I saw in the museum a sculpture of the Peking Man, with his narrow forehead and protruded jaws, I was rather discouraged by the rough-hewn features of primitive humans. The stone tools they had painstakingly crafted looked but crude playthings. We are struck by little toddlers skilfully toying with their words and marvel at how far we have come in human evolution. Our mind is a living history book, in which are imprinted countless steps taken tentatively by our ancestors. None of us is a lone being entire of his or her own, but an offshoot of the ancient tree, at one with Mother Earth, and a link in the endless chain of humanity, each important with a sacred promise which we cannot shirk.

The combination of genes that allowed our life to begin was random and accidental, with infinite possibilities morphing beyond our control. In this sense, each of us is a product of chance. This can put me in a horrid mood, with an inevitable sense of melancholy, fear and uncertainty as to our origin and where we are headed. Yet, I must stop this spiral of sad thoughts. Indeed, our life is what rises to the apex of a pyramid of probabilities — a marvel of nature, a glimpse of the divine, which we have no right to make light of.

To our parents, each of us is unique and precious, no matter how many siblings we may have. Should I ever cease to exist, their love for me would be left with a void, like the loose thread of a spider's web flailing in the air. If I were to fall ill, they would cringe and fervently pray for my quick recovery, to the point of willing to endure suffering in exchange for my well-being. In their eyes, each of my little accomplishments is glorious, cherished in their heart, and magnified like a ray of light through a prism.

If we were to depart before our parents, their grey-haired head would be downcast, and their tears flow no end. When we think of such heart-rending sorrow of unbearable weight, how could we dare to denigrate our importance?

Our memories are so intertwined with those of our better half, like colours of yellow and blue being blended to create a shared green. When a man loses his wife, the pain is that of a heart without protection, naked, bleeding at every slight jolt. When a woman loses her husband, her sorrow is the woeful tune strummed on a mean zither. How could we have the heart to say to our soulmate, "I am not important?"

We mean the world to our children. We are all powerful and irreplaceable like the deep ocean, the whole of their universe. Should we disappear, they would lose inimitable parental love; their sky would fall and world cave in. A broken pot may be mended; a deprived childhood, without a mother's hands to dress bruises and father's wisdom to counsel on tough decisions, can be ruined beyond repair. How could we have the nerve to say to our children, "I am not important?"

With a friend whom I've known for years, I can tell how she feels by the slight twitch of her brow or a batting of her eyelashes. Should I be gone, it would leave a huge void in her heart; a digital file without any duplicate, irretrievable and lost forever. In the still of night, she'd stop abruptly after tapping the first few digits on the phone; numbers that she needn't remember any more. In the holiday season, she'd pause and close her eyes, as she reaches my name in the address book when writing greeting cards. A long moment later and in solitude, she'd put it to flames — the greeting card with only my name and no address on it.

Long-time friends are treasures to behold; like ancient potteries unearthed from a desert site — no replica, no replacement if they were ever broken. How could we have the conceit to say to our friends, "I am not important?"

Yes, I am important. For my work and career, I am indispensable and always in the driver-seat. My innovative, out-of-the-box ideas come forth, like pigeons gliding in the sky, yet homing in to me; like pearls scattered on sand, waiting to be picked up and threaded into a magnificent tapestry. Dedicated to my mission and gazing far ahead, I am of great importance, irreplaceable as I cannot replace anyone else.

I tell myself that I am important, in a small voice, for we have all been so used to brushing away our self-importance and have yet to learn to declare our conviction loudly.

I repeat, "I am important!" This time a little louder. I hear the words resonate, my heart racing, beating more strongly than ever.

Then, I say it out loud for all the world to hear and I hear echoes from distant mountains.

We should all have the courage to say, "I am important." We may be of lowly station or modest with small beginnings. Yet, none of this diminishes our importance.

Importance is not equal to voluminous size, but a reckoning of our life's promise.

We are often judged by the kind of careers we have and our accomplishments. But I want to say that our life is significant and beyond compare, as long as we do not cease our honest work and our struggle for a bright future.

Let us hold our head high and loudly declare to all on this beautiful planet — I am important.

发出声音永远是有用的

如果你遭到了很不公平的对待，请不要抱怨。这个世界就是如此地不平等，在你以前很久，就是这样了。在你以后很久，也会是这样。所以，它等待着你的降临和奋斗。你的降临和奋斗，也许什么也不能改变，也许能让它变得更美好一些，但起码这个世界因为有了你的存在，而有了希望。

有一年，我应邀到一所中学演讲。中国北方的农村，露天操场，围坐着几千名学生。他们穿着翠蓝色校服，脸蛋呈现出一种深紫的玫瑰红色。冬天，很冷。事先，我曾问过校方，不能找个暖和点的地方吗？校长为难地说，乡下学校，都是这种条件，凡是开全校大会，都在操场上。我说，其实不是在考虑自己，而是想孩子们可受得了。校长说，您放宽心好了，没事。农村孩子，抗冻着呢。

我从不曾在这样冷的地方讲过这么多的话。虽然，我以前在西藏待过，经历过零下四十摄氏度的严寒，但那时军人们急匆匆像木偶一般赶路，缄口不语，说话会让周身的热量非常快地流失。这一次，吸进冷风，呼出热气，在腊月的严寒中面对着一群眼巴巴的农村少年谈人生和理想，我口中吐冒一团的白烟，像老式的蒸汽火车头。

演讲完了，我说，谁有什么问题，可以写张字条。这是演讲的惯例，我有什么地方说得不妥当，请人家指正。孩子们掏出纸笔，往手心哈一口热气，纷纷写起来。老师只是很负责地在操场上穿行，收集字条。

我打开一张字条。上面写着：我很生气，这个世界是不平等的。比如，我为什么是一个女孩呢？我的爸爸为什么是一个农民，而我同桌的爸爸却是县长？为什么我上学要走那么远的路，我的同桌却坐着小汽车？为什么我只有一支笔，他却有那么大的一个铅笔盒……

我看着那一排钩子一样的问号，心想这是一个充满了愤怒的

发出声音永远是有用的

女孩，如果她张嘴说话，一定像冲出了一股乙炔，空气都会燃起蓝白的火苗。

我大声地把她的条子念了出来。那一瞬，操场上很静很静，听得见遥远的天边，有一只小鸟在嘹亮地歌唱。我从台子上望下去，一双双乌溜溜的眼珠，在玫瑰红色的脸蛋上瞪得溜圆。还有人东张西望，估计他们在猜测字条的主人。

据说孩子们在妈妈的肚子里，就能体会到母亲的感情。很多女孩子从那个时候，就感受到了这个世界的不平等，因为你不是一个男孩，你不符合大家的期望。

这有什么办法吗？没有。起码在现阶段，没有办法改变你的性别。你只有认命。我在这里说的"命"，不是虚无缥缈的命运，而是指你与生俱来的一些不能改变的东西。比如你的性别，比如你的相貌，比如你的父母，比如你降生的时间地点……总之，在你出生以前就已经具备的这些东西，都不是你所能左右的。你只能安然接受。

不要相信别人对你说的这个世界是平等的那些话。在现阶段，这只是一厢情愿。不过，你不必悲观丧气。其实，世界已经渐渐在向平等的灯塔航行。比如一百年前，你能到学堂里来读书吗？你很可能裹着小脚，在屋里低眉顺眼地学做女红。县长的儿子，在那个时候，要叫作县太爷的公子了，你怎么可能和他成为同桌？在争取平等的路上，我们已经出发了。

没有什么人承诺和担保你一生下来就享有阳光灿烂的平等。你去看看动物界，就知道平等是多么罕见了。平等是人类智慧的产物，是维持最大多数人安宁的策略。你明白了这件事情，就会少很多愤怒，多很多感恩。你已经享受了很多人奋斗的成果，你的回报就是继续努力，而不是抱怨。

身为女子，你不要对这样的不平等安之若素，你可以发出声音。说了和没有说，在暂时的结果上可能是一样的，但长远的感受和影响是不一样的，对你性格的发展是不一样的。而且，只要你不断地说下去，事情也许就会有变化。记住，发出声音永远是有用的，因为它们可能会被听到并引发改变。

说实话，让一个受到忽视的女孩子，很小就发出对于自己不公平待遇的呐喊，几乎是不可能的。但我思索再三，还是决定保留这个期望。因为今天的女子，也可能变成明天的母亲。如若她们因循守旧，照样端起了不平等的衣钵，如若她们的女儿发出呼声，也许能触动她们内在的记忆，事情就有可能发生变化。当然了，如果女孩子长大了，到了公共场合，这一条就更要记住并择机实施。记住，呐喊是必需的，就算这一辈子无人听见，回声也将激荡久远。

Speaking-Out Matters

Don't complain when you are treated unfairly. Life is unfair. That's the way it is and will always be in the world. Your existence and your strife may make it a better place than it was, or change nothing at all. But there is at least hope since you are in this world.

I was once invited to give a talk at a rural high school in northern China. Several thousand students in bright blue uniforms assembled in the schoolyard on a wintry day, ruddy in the face because of the cold. I had asked earlier if it could be held somewhere warmer. Flustered, the headmaster said that was all they could manage and it was the same in all rural schools without a school auditorium — assemblies being held outdoors. I said I was not thinking of myself, but the pupils who had to listen to me talk in the extreme cold. The headmaster assured me that they were all rural kids and the cold would be nothing to them.

I had never had to talk at length outside in the freezing cold. In my years in Tibet where temperatures in winter regularly plunged below minus 40 degrees Celsius, we went about our business outdoors as soldiers with our mouths shut, scurrying like stiff, mum marionettes, so as not to lose body heat quickly. Now, on this cold day in the coldest month of the year, I puffed, cold air in and warm breath out, sending off billowing vapours as if an old steam engine, as I rambled on about life and ideal to the crowd of eager teenagers from the villages.

When I wound up my talk, I asked the students

to write down any questions or comments they might have on a slip of paper. This had also been my way of getting feedback. So, the students took out their pencils and paper and began scribbling, after blowing on their hands to warm up their stiff fingers. The teachers circulated to collect the paper slips.

The first note I opened said, "I am angry at the world. Life is so unfair. For example, why should I have been born a girl? Why is my father a farmer while my desk-mate's the county mayor? Why do I have to walk for miles to get to school while he arrives in a car? Why do I have only one pencil while he a boxful?"

The question marks stood out like crooked barbs. I imagined this to be a girl, fuming with wrath. Had she spoken then, words would have gushed out, like puffs of acetylene that could burn with a blazing blue flame.

After I read her note aloud, the assembly fell quiet; so quiet I could hear a little bird chirping far, far away. From the raised platform, my eyes roved over the assembly, meeting the pupils' that were peeled, black and shiny like pebbles, against their ruddy cheeks. A few heads turned, in search of its likely author.

It is said that babies can feel their mom's emotions in the womb. Many baby girls must have thus felt the prejudice of the world, for they were deemed to have let others down because of their gender.

Is there anything you can do? No, you cannot change you gender, at least for now. You are so destined and you have to live with it. By destiny I do not mean anything metaphysical, but what comes with birth — your gender, looks, parents, the time and place of your birth — which you cannot change. In short, you must accept anything that had been there before your birth.

Don't believe those who say there is already gender equality. It is only wishful thinking. However, you shouldn't be discouraged either, for society is steadily moving towards that goal. A century ago, all girls were denied schooling, and had to have their feet bound and start practicing needlework from an early age. If it were a century ago, the county mayor's son would have been a minor princeling and there would have been no chance for a girl to share a desk with him. Our move to equality is well underway.

There is no such a thing as everyone being born equal. Equality is not a natural right; you need look no further than the animal kingdom. Equality is a notion arising out of wisdom — a strategy for keeping the majority tranquil and peaceful. When you get to grips with this, you will feel less anger and more gratitude. You are already enjoying the fruits of others' strife and what you should do in return is working harder and not to complain.

As a female, you should of course not turn a blind eye to gender inequality. Speak out when you see unfairness. It may very well not make a dent immediately, but will have a positive impact on your character in the long run. As you keep doing this, things may truly change. Remember, speaking out matters, for you will eventually be heard and effect change.

To be honest, it may be nearly impossible for a young girl, neglected, to speak out against unfair treatment. Yet I still hold such a hope after thinking about it long and hard. A girl today may well be a mother tomorrow. Her submission now will encourage more inequality. Her loud voice will kindle what is buried deep in memory. Then change will occur. She should keep in mind that as she grows up and interact with others in society at large, she must speak out when the occasion requires. It is something she must do. Even if no one ever takes notice, her voice will have powerful and lingering echoes.

行使拒绝权

拒绝是一种权利，就像生存是一种权利。

古人说，有所不为才能有所为。这个"不为"，就是拒绝。人们常常以为拒绝是一种迫不得已的防卫，殊不知它更是一种主动的选择。

纵观我们的一生，选择拒绝的机会，实在比选择赞成的机会要多得多。因为生命属于我们的只有一次，要用唯一的生命成就一种事业，就需在千条道路中寻觅仅有的花径。我们确定了"一"，就拒绝了九百九十九。

拒绝如影随形，是我们一生不可拒绝的密友。

我们无时无刻不是生活在拒绝之中，它出现的频率，远较我们想象的频繁。

你穿起红色的衣服，就是拒绝了红色以外所有的衣服。

你今天上午选择了读书，就是拒绝了唱歌跳舞，拒绝了参观旅游，拒绝了与朋友的聊天，拒绝了和对手的谈判……拒绝了支配这段时间的其他种种可能。

你的午餐是馒头和炒菜，你的胃就等于庄严宣布同米饭、饺子、馅饼和各式各样的煲汤绝缘。无论你怎样逼迫它也是枉然，因为它容积有限。

你选择了律师这个职业，毫无疑问就等于拒绝了建筑师的头衔。也许一个世纪以前，同一块土地还可套种，精力过人的智者还可多方向出击，游刃有余。随着现代社会的发展，任何一行都需从业者的全力以赴，除非你天分极高，否则兼做的最大可能性，是在两条战线功败垂成。

你认定了一个男人或是一个女人为终身伴侣，就斩钉截铁地拒绝了这世界上数以亿计的其他男人或女人，也许他们更坚毅、更美丽，但拒绝就是取消，拒绝就是否决，拒绝使你一劳永逸，拒绝让你义无反顾，拒绝在给予你自由的同时，取缔了你更多的自由。拒绝是一条单行道，你开启了闸门，江河就奔涌而去，无法回头。

拒绝对我们如此重要，我们在拒绝中成长和奋进。如果你不会拒绝，你就无法成功地跨越生命。

拒绝的实质是一种否定性的选择。

拒绝的时候，我们往往显得过于匆忙。

我们在有可能从容拒绝的日子里，胆怯而迟疑地挥霍了光阴。我们推迟拒绝，我们惧怕拒绝。我们把拒绝比作困境中的背水一战，只要有一分可能，就鸵鸟似的缩进沙砾。殊不知当我们选择拒绝的时候，更应该冷静和周全，更应有充分的时间分析利弊与后果。拒绝应该是慎重思虑之后一枚成熟的浆果，而不是强行捋下的酸葡萄。

拒绝的本质是一种丧失，它与温柔热烈的赞同相比，折射出冷峻的付出与掷地有声的清脆，更需要果决的判断和一往无前的勇气。

你拒绝了金钱，就将毕生扼守清贫。

你拒绝了享乐，就将布衣素食、天涯苦旅。

你拒绝了父母，就可能成为飘零的小舟，孤悬海外。

你拒绝了师长，就可能被逐出师门，自生自灭。

你拒绝了上司，也许意味着与一个如花似锦的前程分道扬镳。

你拒绝了机遇，它永不再回头光顾你一眼，留下终身的遗憾任你咀嚼。

拒绝不像选择那样令人心情舒畅，它森严的外衣里裹着我们始料不及的风刀霜剑，像一种后劲很大的烈酒，在漫长的夜晚使我们头晕目眩。

于是我们本能地惧怕拒绝。我们在无数应该说"不"的场合沉默，我们在理应拒绝的时刻延宕不决。我们推迟拒绝的那一刻，梦想拒绝的体积会随着时光的流逝逐渐缩小以至消失。

可惜这只是我们善良的愿望，真实的情境往往适得其反。我们之所以拒绝，是因为我们不得不拒绝。

不拒绝，那本该被拒绝的事物，就像菜花状的癌肿蓬蓬勃勃地生长、浸润，侵袭我们的生命，一天比一天更加难以救治。

拒绝是苦，然而那是一时之苦，阵痛之后便是安宁。

不拒绝是忍，心字上面一把刀。忍是有限度的，到了忍无可忍的那一刻，贻误的是时间，收获的是更大的痛苦与麻烦。

拒绝是对一个人胆魄和心智的考验。

拒绝是一门艺术。

拒绝也分阳刚派与阴柔派。

怒发冲冠是拒绝，浅吟低唱也是拒绝。义正词严是拒绝，

"顾左右而言他"也是拒绝。声色俱厉是拒绝，低眉敛目也是拒绝。横刀跃马是拒绝，丝弦管竹也是拒绝。

只要心意决绝，无论何方舞台，都可演成拒绝的绝唱。

拒绝有时候需要借口。

借口是一层薄薄的帷幕。它更多表达的是一种善意、一种心情，而同表面的含义无关。

借口悬挂于双方之间，使我们彼此听得见拒绝清脆的声音，看不见拒绝淡漠的表情，因此维持着最后的礼仪。

许多被拒绝的人，执着地追问理由，以为驳倒了理由就挽救了拒绝。这实在是一种淡淡的愚蠢，理由是生长在拒绝这棵大树上取之不尽、用之不竭的叶子。如果你真的是想挽回拒绝，就去给大树浇水吧。

在某种程度上，借口会销蚀拒绝的力度。它把人们的注意力牵扯到无关的细节，而忽略了坚硬的内核。就像过多的糖稀，会损坏牙齿的珐琅质。它混淆了拒绝真实凝重的本色，使原本简单的事物斑驳不清。

相较之下，我更喜欢那种干干净净没有任何赘物的斩钉截铁地拒绝，它像北方三九天的冰凌，有一种肝胆相照的晶莹和砰然断裂的爽快。不但是个人意志的伸张，而且是给予对方的信任和尊崇。

天下无数繁杂的道路，你只能走一条。你若是条条都走，那就等于在原地转圈子。

拒绝卑微，走向崇高。

拒绝不平，争取公道。

拒绝无端的蔑视和可恶的恩惠，凭自己的双手和头颅挺身立于性别之林。

因为拒绝，我们将伤害一些人，这就像春风必将吹尽落红一样，有时是一种必然。如果我们始终不拒绝，我们就不会伤害别人，但是我们伤害了一个跟自己更亲密的人，那就是我们自己。

拒绝的味道并不可口，当我们鼓起勇气拒绝以后，忧郁和惆怅伴随着我们，一种灵魂被挤压的感觉，久久挥之不去。

因为惧怕这种难以言说的感觉，我们有意无意地减少了拒绝。

在人生所有的决定里，拒绝是属于破坏而难以弥补的粉碎性行为。这一特质决定了我们在做出拒绝的时候，需要格外的镇定与慎重。

然而拒绝一旦做出，就像打破了的牛奶杯，再不会复原。它凝固在我们的脚步里，无论正确与否，都不必原地长久停留。

　　拒绝是没有过错的，该负责任的是我们在拒绝前做出的判断。不必害怕拒绝，我们只需更周密的决断。

　　拒绝是一种删繁就简，拒绝是一种举重若轻。拒绝是一种大智若愚，拒绝是一种水落石出。

　　当利益像万花筒一般使你眼花缭乱之时，你会在混沌之中模糊了视线，尝试一下拒绝吧。

　　你依次拒绝那些自己最不喜欢的人和事，自己的真爱就像退潮时的礁岩，嶙峋地凸现出来，等待你的攀缘。

　　当你抱怨时间像被无数餐刀分割的蛋糕，再也找不到属于你自己的那朵奶油花时，尝试一下拒绝吧。

　　你把所有可做可不做的事拒绝掉，时间就像湿毛巾里的水，一滴一滴地拧出来了。

　　当你发现生活中蕴涵着太多的苦恼，已经迫近一个人能够忍受的极限，情绪在崩溃的边缘时，尝试一下拒绝吧。

你也许会发现，你以前不敢拒绝，是因为怕增添烦恼。但是恰恰相反，拒绝像一柄巨大的梳子，快速地理顺了杂乱无章的日子，使天空恢复明朗。

当你被陀螺般旋转的日子搅得耳鸣目眩，忘记了自己是从哪里来、要到哪里去的时候，尝试一下拒绝吧。

你会惊讶地发觉自己从复杂的包装中清醒，唤起久已枯萎的童心，感叹我们每一个人都是自然之子。

拒绝犹如断臂，带有旧情不再的痛楚。

拒绝犹如狂飙突进，孕育天马横空的独行。

拒绝有时是一首挽歌，回荡袅袅的哀伤。

拒绝更是破釜沉舟的勇气，一种直面淋漓鲜血、惨淡人生的气概。

拒绝也不可太多，假如什么都拒绝，就从根本上拒绝了每个人只有一次的辉煌生命。

智慧地、勇敢地行使拒绝权。

这是我们每个人与生俱来的权利，这是我们意志之舟劈风斩浪的白帆。

Say "No" Bravely and Wisely

To refuse is a right, like that to survival.

"Only by refraining from some actions can we truly accomplish what we desire," as an ancient saying goes. Refusal is often deemed passive defence, but in truth, a choice.

In life, a refusal is in order more often than acquiescence. We have but one life to live and success in any career requires lifelong, single-minded dedication. When we opt for a singular path out of a thousand options, we have rejected nine hundred and ninety-nine others.

To refuse is something we do almost all the time, though not always in a plain and obvious manner. To refuse is to live, which occurs more frequently than we like to imagine.

When you put on a red dress, you have rejected all other colour options. When you choose to read in the morning, you have rejected singing, dancing, going out, chatting with friends or negotiating with your counterpart   ... all other options for the morning.

When you pick steamed buns and stir-fried dishes for lunch, your stomach will have nothing to do with rice, dumplings, pies and soups of all flavours, no matter how appealing they can be, for it will have no room.

If you decide to pursue a legal career, you have shunned the possibility, for example, of being an architect. A century ago, a person of above-average talent could be comfortably proficient in everything that tickled his fancy, becoming a jack of all trades or even a renaissance man, like multiple cropping in farming. Nowadays, it requires total dedication to succeed in one career, and any attempt at multiple paths would be doomed unless you are truly exceptionally talented.

When you have chosen someone as your life partner, you

have turned away from all others, and resolutely at that, even though they may be more audacious or prettier, and number in the millions. What's done is done; turning away is firm rejection. It puts your mind at ease, allowing you to be totally dedicated. While giving you the freedom to refuse, it also takes away the freedom to use any options other than the one chosen. Rejection is a one-way path, a channel with water running in one direction, once the floodgate is open.

To refuse is critical to growth and progress. If you do not refuse, you could not overcome obstacles and succeed in life. To refuse is negation by deliberate choice.

However, we are often in a hurry when we refuse, because we have been coy and hesitant, dallying when rejection can be done at our leisure. We keep putting it off, for we are daunted by it, seeing it as the last resort. We avoid it while we can, like an ostrich with its head in the sand. Little do we know that rejection is best done in a coolheaded manner, with ample time for deliberation and weighing the pros and cons, so that our choice is like a ripe berry, rather than a tart grape.

To refuse also means to discard, which, unlike cordial acceptance, must be done in an unsentimental, resolute, and unequivocal manner, allowing no change of heart.

When you reject the pursuit of money, you will live a life of poverty.

When you reject hedonism, you opt for a life of simplicity, like a nomad on the fringe.

When you reject your parents, you are forlorn, like a lonely skiff out in the vast sea.

When you part ways with your mentors or masters, you are stripped of their tutelage and utterly on your own. When you disobey your superiors, you have shunned the prospect of an otherwise gainful career. When you chivalrously turn down an opportunity, it will never knock again, leaving you to regret for the rest of your life.

You never really enjoy the act of rejection, as you do acceptance. You may find to your surprise that it can be absolutely agonizing, like a bitter pill to swallow, or a hard liquor that makes you tipsy while the night is long and guarantees a painful hangover.

Thus, by instinct, we fear rejection, keeping mum time and again when we should have said "No." We defer when we have every reason to reject outright. While dilly-dallying, our resolve to reject wane and disappear in time.

Unfortunately, rejection can often be the choice that we had to make. If we don't, what should have been rejected will get out of hand, like a tumour, cauliflower-like, relentlessly invading our body until we are beyond remedy.

Rejection can be painful. Yet, the pain will come to pass, after which peace ensues. Rejection postponed only causes greater pain down the road, as forbearance is pushed beyond limits and time lost.

Rejection tests a person's valour, nerve and intellect. Rejection comes in myriad forms, akin to art, with muscular and feminine styles. Rejection can be raw fury or a soothing tune; a stern, righteous snub or hemming and hawing; a hysteric roar or a hushed mumble; fighting cheek by jowl or trite platitudes. With one's mind made up, rejection can be rendered in any way one sees fit.

Sometimes, rejection needs a pretext, which more often than not conveys a kindly sentiment. The pretext itself is but a veil that softens the harshness of a clear rebuttal and keeps the appearance of courtesy.

Many on the receiving end, when given the pretext, insisted on getting to the bottom of it. They believed that if somehow they could refute the pretext itself, they might save the day. This is rather dumb, for those who refuse may come up with numerous excuses. If you really care, turn to the cause rather than pretexts.

To some extent, a pretext may diminish the force of

rejection, drawing attention to irrelevant details and away from the core. A pretext can confuse others as to the weighty crux of the matter. It may help the medicine go down, yet too much sugar may damage the enamel of the teeth, too.

Therefore, I much prefer outright, resolute rejection, without all the bells and whistles. Rejection done in this manner is transparent and clear-cut, like icicles hanging from the eaves in a northern Chinese winter — sharp, crystalline, breaking clear when shaken. It reflects at once one's resolve and respect for anyone on the receiving end of a rejection.

Of all the possible paths on earth, you are to take only one, or else you would be turning round in circles.

So, reject the mean-spirited and opt for the noble. Reject unfairness and fight for justice. Reject vile favouritism and prejudice, and stand up for the opportunity to compete on equal footing with others regardless of gender.

We may hurt others when rejecting, which is only natural, like the winds plucking off flowers in spring. If we never refuse, we may spare ourselves the agony of hurting others, but will hurt instead ourselves — who are dearer to us.

Rejection is never pleasant. Hardly have we summoned enough courage to reject when we begin to feel a sense of loss and melancholy, and a twinge of dejection that refuses to go away. Averse to such an unspeakable mixture of feelings, we refrain from rejecting, sometimes in spite of ourselves.

Of all the decisions that one makes in life, rejection is of the kind that is irreparably destructive. Because of this, we need to be cautious and cool-headed when making the decision, for once a refusal is made, there is no turning back — like a glass broken, beyond repair or a step taken beyond the point of no return.

While rejection is unequivocal, the judgement that precipitates it is subject to deliberation. Although we need not fear to refuse, we need careful, prior contemplation.

Rejection reflects an approximation to simplicity, masterfulness, uncanny wisdom and clairvoyance. Practise the art of rejection when temptation dazzles you like a kaleidoscope of a thousand illusions.

Only when you have rejected individuals and preoccupations that you detest can you devote yourself to your true passion which becomes all the more prominent — a submerged reef revealed as the tide recedes.

When you complain about your time being taken up by and wasted on frivolities, why don't you try rejection? When you push aside all frivolous preoccupations, time becomes available, like water being wrung out of a wet rag.

Try rejection when you feel that your life is a tale of endless sorrow, and that you are at the end of your tether and on the brink of collapse.

You may have refrained from rejecting for fear of more self-inflicted anguish and agony. Rejection, on the contrary, has a tremendous cleansing power, eliminating the unnecessary and bringing order to, and brightening up, your life.

Try rejection when you have lost your bearing in life, going through the daily grind, feeling as though you were being whipped endlessly like a spinning top. As your long buried passion and child-like wonder is reawakened, you will be surprised to find that we are all children of Mother Nature.

Rejection must be resolute, with pain and anguish like that of leaving your lover.

Rejection is a storm, a hurricane, requiring the unfettered bravery of a lone knight errant.

Rejection is a swansong, with a tinge of grief.

Rejection means burning all bridges without regret or remorse in the face of the bleak adversity in life.

However, rejection is no card blanche; if you reject all the time and everywhere you go, you'd reject life altogether — life that we live but once.

Therefore reject bravely and wisely. It is our natural right — giving us resolute force, like the sail allowing the vessel to plough the waves on the high seas.

自卑情结是幸福的最大敌人

有一种天然的感觉，伴随我们一生。有人说，那是爱，其实不是。爱不是天生就具备的品德，是需要学习的。一个刚刚出生的婴儿，并不懂得爱，但他感到了自卑。哭声就是自卑的旗帜，那是对寒冷（相比于母体内的恒温）、对孤独（相比于母体内的依傍）的第一声惊恐的告白，也是被迫独立生活的宣言。这个景象挺有象征意义。人在强大的自然规律面前，没有法子不自卑。但是，人类不能被自卑打倒，人就是在同自卑的抗争中成长壮大起来的。

可以说，自卑是幸福的最大敌人。道理很简单，一个人若是时时事事都沉浸在自卑中，那他如何还能享受幸福？

所以，人不要被自卑打垮，而是要超越自卑。咱们先来找找自卑的反义词是什么。我小时候，很喜欢"找反义词"这类题目，在寻找中，你对原本的那个词有了更深入的了解，就像黑和白站在一起，一定显出黑的更黑、白的更白。只有在黑暗中，你才能看到所有的光。如果黑和灰站在一起，就容易混淆。

自卑的反义词是自信。自卑和自信，都有一个"自"，就是"自己"的意思。那么，自己对待自己，有什么不同呢？自卑的人，自己看不起自己；自信的人，自己相信自己。从这里入手，我们就找到了自卑和自信最显著的分水岭，那就是，一事当前，自信的人说，我能做这件事；自卑的人会说，我办不成这件事。

面对一生，自信的人说：我能成为理想中那样的人，我要掌握自己的命运。

自卑的人会说：我不能成为自己想成为的那样的人，我只能随波逐流，被外力摆布。

"自卑"这个词，平日里大家说得很多，但究竟什么是自卑呢？自卑有哪些表现呢？自卑为什么会成为幸福的大敌呢？

简言之，自卑就是有关自我的消极信念，影响了成长。

记得儿时读过《好兵帅克》这部小说，里面有个人物，特别喜欢求本溯源。比如他说到窗户，就要说窗户是木头做的，他马上就会接下来解释，木头是树木，那树木又是从哪里来的呢？它们来自森林……现在我们谈到自卑，多少也陷入了这种论证的漫长小径。有点儿啰唆，请原谅。

自卑的人，充满了对自己的不良观念和不适宜的评价。自卑的要害是——自我否定。看看"否"这个字，"口"上面是个"不"字，一个人一张口就吐出"不"来。人是需要说"不"的，不知道说"不"的人，一生太辛劳，完全丧失了自我。但是，如果一个人一辈子说"不"太多，尤其是对自己总是说"不"，那就成了大问题。

最详细地论证了自卑这种情绪的是个体心理学的创始人阿德勒，他发现了一个自卑情结。

阿德勒是一位奥地利精神病学家，被称为"现代自我心理学之父"。他于一八七〇年出生在维也纳的一个商人家庭，排行老二。家境富裕，家人都很喜欢音乐，按说这是一个丰衣足食的幸福环境，可是，童年的阿德勒一点儿也不快乐。为什么呢？原因来自他的亲哥哥。两人虽是一母所生，但哥哥高大健壮，活蹦乱跳，人见人爱，阿德勒却自小体弱多病，还是个驼背。他五岁那年，又生了一场大病，更让他身材矮小、面容丑陋。好在阿德勒很聪明，后来他考入大学，毕业后当了医生。由于自身的残疾，一九〇七年，他发表了有关由身体缺陷引发自卑的论文，从此声名大噪。他不赞成弗洛伊德的性决定论，强调社会文化因素在人格形成和发展中的决定性作用。他的主要观点是：追求卓越是人类动机的核心，而如何追求卓越，则取决于每个人独特的生活风格。追求卓越是一种天生的内驱力，使人力图成为一个没有缺陷的人、一个完善的人。人总是有缺陷的，由于身体或其他原因引发的自卑，能摧毁一个人，使人自甘堕落或得精神病，另一方面，它还能使人发愤图强，力求振作，以弥补自己的缺点。

比如说，古希腊的德摩斯梯尼，小时候患有口吃，可他迎难而上，刻苦锻炼，最后成了著名的演说家。美国的罗斯福，患有小儿麻痹症，但他最终成为美国总统。尼采身体羸弱，他就研究权力哲学，成了一代大哲学家。

Inferiority, the Nemesis of Happiness

There is a feeling that follows a person the day he is born. Some may say it is love. However, love is learned, not something congenital. A newborn knows nothing about love, but feels helpless and insecure. His first cries express his fears more than anything else, when he feels cold and alone, in contrast to being warm and cosy inside the womb. They are symbolic of humanity's feelings of inferiority when exposed to the elements and forces of nature. Yet, humans should not be defeated by such a sense of inferiority; it is by vowing to overcome it that humans grow strong.

Inferiority is the nemesis of happiness, for a person who

seethes with angst and inferiority, he has no happiness to speak of, plain and simple.

We should rise above, and not be crushed by inferiority. To begin with, let us look at the opposite of inferiority. Back in my time, I had always enjoyed the schoolwork of looking up antonyms for words. In so doing, I gained a deeper understanding of them. When a word is placed alongside its antonyms, its meaning becomes clearer, by comparison and contrast, as the flicker of light stands out in the darkness of night. The antonym for inferiority complex is self-esteem. Both involve self-perception. He who is consumed with inferiority lacks confidence, while he who has self-esteem is assured of his true worth. When presented with a challenge, the latter says "I can" while the former "I can't."

In their outlook on life, a man of self-esteem, taking destiny in his own hands, believes he can become the person he aspires to be, while a man of insecurity thinks he will never be the person he wants to be, resigning to go with the flow, at the mercy of powers beyond his own.

Inferiority complex is often heard in common parlance. But what is it exactly? Why is it the nemesis of happiness?

In short, inferiority complex arises out of a persistent, negative self-perception, which adversely affects one's development.

People with low self-esteem suffer from a negative and inappropriate appraisal of themselves. The essence of inferiority is self-negation. The Chinese ideogram for "negation（否）" consists of two parts — mouth and no. Of course, one needs to say "no" when it is necessary and appropriate. To never refuse is to be unkind and harsh to oneself. Yet if one says "no" too often, and in particular, always to oneself, then there is a problem.

Alfred Adler, founder of the school of individual psychology, discovered what he called inferiority complex after extensive studies of feelings of inferiority. An Austrian psychotherapist, the father of ego psychology, he was born in 1870, the second child to a Viennese merchant and his wife. Although his family was prosperous and music-loving, Alfred was not happy in his childhood. It was because he lived in the shadow of his elder brother who was tall, strong, active and popular, while Alfred small, with average looks and suffering from rickets from early on. At the age of five, he was stricken by a serious illness that further hindered his physical growth. Yet, Alfred was a smart kid and eventually got into medical college and became a physician. His own deformities led to his publications of treatises on "organ inferiorities" and inferiority complex in 1907, to great acclaim. He did not share Freud's views and contended that social and cultural influences, rather than libido, drove the development of personality. His main argument was that the pursuit of self ideal was the core motivational force in human behaviour, and such pursuits varied according to each individual's lifestyle. An individual has the natural, innate urge to channel feelings of inferiority into an endeavour to achieve superiority, excellence and perfection.

Given our inevitable deficiencies, the accompanying sense of inferiority can be self-destructive, leading to indolence and even mental illness. On the other hand, acknowledging inferiority and vowing to overcome it can be a powerful force, helping us compensate our deficiencies.

For example, Demosthenes of ancient Greece became a renowned orator, after overcoming his speech impediment with strenuous training and practice. Franklin D. Roosevelt became the US President despite being crippled by polio. Nietzsche, who was plagued by disruptive illnesses and poor health, became a great philosopher of his time, with studies on the will to power.

击碎无所不在的尺

以最平凡的态度，做最不平凡的事情，这就是"平常心"的真谛了。

"平常心"这几个字，说的人多，真正明白的人没有那么多。因为"平常"，并不是听之任之随波逐流，它是一种务实而踏实的人生态度，并不像我们想象的那样容易，是高度智慧的不经意表现，是坚强意志的莞尔一笑。

如果别人对你没有要求，其实是很惨的事情。你被放逐了，你会觉得无价值感，会丧失了归属感。所以，当别人对你有很高要求的时候，你不必沮丧。

那正是他高看你的能力，以为你能够胜任。当然了，如果确实超出了你的范畴，你可以提出看法，但不必垂头丧气。

到处是尺。尺度要人命。身高是尺，因为它赫然列在征婚条件的前几行。体重是尺，因为它和很多人的自我形象密切相关。职务是尺，简直就是衡量你是否进步的唯一阶梯。排名是尺，无论在国际上还是在国内省内校内班内，都是你的资格和位置的标杆。然而，设立尺的那个人是谁？人们已经忘记。

把自己从尺度中救出来，是当务之急。

永远不要把别人的进步，当成衡量你自己有无能力的尺度。那是不自信的人惯用的方式。无论是对自己还是对别人，万勿期望太高。所以，同学聚会的时候，你尽管放松，我们因为过去的友谊而重逢，这并不是今日近况的比武场。

Never Live by Others' Yardsticks

He who is humble, yet accomplishes extraordinary things, is truly the salt of the earth.

We talk about the salt of the earth often without understanding what it really means. It is a pragmatic, down-to-earth attitude to life, emblematic of superior wisdom and will of steel, natural and uncontrived. It has nothing to do with being wishy-washy and going with the flow.

Not being needed is a rather dismal feeling. You are in limbo, deprived of any sense of belonging and see little worth in yourself. Therefore, never fret when others expect much of you. They do so because they hold you in high regard and believe that you are superbly capable. Of course, if such expectations are beyond what you can deliver, you could simply let them know, rather than be bothered and glum.

We face expectations everywhere. They often become rules that can also be limiting and even deadly. For example, you are expected to be tall and shapely as a marriage prospect. Weight, too, can be a measure, vital to the self-esteem of many. The job title you carry marks your rung on the ladder, sometimes being the only measure of success for some. The ranking of your college, your school, and your own ranking in your class mark your academic standing. With myriad yardsticks everywhere, nobody remembers why you must be judged by them in the first place.

You must extricate yourself from the confines of these yardsticks.

Never use others' achievements as a yardstick for your own capability; it is a common pitfall of those with low self-esteem. Do not have unreasonably high expectations of yourself or others. Relax and enjoy yourself at your next school reunion, for this should be the occasion for renewing old friendships, not comparing notes on how we have fared in the world.

我羡慕你

我是从哪一天开始老的？不知道。就像从夏到秋，人们只觉得天气一天一天凉了，却说不出秋天究竟是哪一天来到的。生命的"立秋"是从哪一个生日开始的？不知道。青年的年龄上限不断提高，我有时觉得那都是上了年纪的人玩出的花样，为掩饰自己的衰老，便总说别人年轻。

不管怎么样，我觉得自己老了。当别人问我年龄的时候，我支支吾吾地反问一句，您看我有多大了？佯装的镇定当中，希望别人说出的数字要较我实际年龄稍小一些。倘若人家说得过小了，又暗暗怀疑那人是否在成心奚落。我开始越来越多地照镜子。小说中常说年轻的姑娘们最爱照镜子，其实那是不正确的。年轻人不必照镜子，世人羡慕他们的目光就是镜子，真正开始细细端详自己的容貌的是青春将逝的人们。

于是我把所有的精力放在孩子身上。记得一个秋天的早晨，刚下夜班的我强打精神，带着儿子去公园。儿子在铺满卵石的小路上走着，他踩着甬路旁镶着的花砖一蹦一跳地向前跑，将我越甩越远。

走中间的平路！我大声地对他呼喊。

不！妈妈！我喜欢……他头也不回地答道。

我蓦地站住了，这句话是那样熟悉。曾几何时，我也这样对自己的妈妈说过，我喜欢在不平坦的路上行走。这一切过去得多么快呀！从哪一天开始，我行动的步伐开始减慢，我越来越多地抱怨起路的不平了呢？

这是衰老确凿无疑的证据。岁月不可逆转，我不会再年轻了。

孩子，我羡慕你！我吓了一跳。这是实实在在的声音，从我身后传来，说得很缓慢，好像我的大脑变成一块电视屏幕，任何人都能读出上面的字幕。

我转过身。身后是一位老年妇女，周围再没有其他人。这么说，是她羡慕我。我仔细打量着她，头发花白，衣着普通。但她有一种气质，虽说身材瘦小，却有一种令人仰视的感觉。我疑惑地看着她，我不知道自己有什么值得人羡慕的地方，一个工厂里刚下夜班满脸疲惫之色的女人。

是的。我羡慕你的年纪，你们的年纪。她用手指轻轻点了点，将远处我儿子越来越小的身影也括了进去，我愿意用我所获得过的一切，来换你现在的年纪。

我至今不知道她是谁，不知道她曾经获得过的那一切都是些什么，但我感谢她让我看到了自己拥有的财富。我们常常过多地注视别人，而自己在不知不觉中失去了最宝贵的东西。人的生命是一根链条，永远有比你年轻的孩子和比你年迈的老人，我们每个人都有自己的位置，有一宗谁也掠夺不去的财宝。不要计较何时年轻，何时年老。只要我们生存一天，青春的财富就闪闪发光。能够遮蔽它的光芒的暗夜只有一种，那就是你自以为已经衰老。

年轻的朋友，不要去羡慕别人。要记住人们在羡慕我们！

159

Hey, I Envy You

When did I start getting old? I have not a clue. The seasons turn and the autumn is in the air, yet no one knows exactly when it started. On which of your birthdays does the autumn of life fall? The upper border of "being young" has been pushed up repeatedly. I sometimes wonder if it was some trick that older people trying to pull — hinting that they have yet to be old by saying everyone else are still young.

Regardless, I do feel I am getting on in years. When others boldly enquired about my age of late, I'd dodge and retort with feigned airiness, "How old do you think?" I'd be secretly pining for a figure lower than my actual age, but not too low, lest I'd suspect ridicule. I began to look at myself in the mirror more often. Young girls are portrayed in fictions as being fond of staring at themselves in the mirror, which is not true. They have little use of mirrors. They see their own reflections in the eyes of others. Once you find yourself starting to examine your countenance in the mirror, youth is on the wane.

So I devoted most of my energy to my son. I remember one autumn morning when I took him to the park, struggling to be cheerful after a night shift. He trotted ahead on the footpath paved with river pebbles and hopped playfully on the decorative pavers along the edge, as I dropped behind.

"Stay on the flat path in the middle!" I shouted after him.

"No, Mom! I like the uneven ..." he shouted back without turning his head.

His reply, with a harrowing ring of familiarity, stopped me in my tracks. It seemed only a short while ago that I said the same to my mother — "I like walking on the uneven surface." Decades had passed. I couldn't recall when I started my slower gait and complaining about walkways being not as even as they should be.

It was proof beyond any doubt that I had started getting old. You cannot turn back the clock, reverse the passing of years. You will not be young any more.

"Hey, how I envy you!" A voice that came from behind gave me a jolt. The words were deliberate and slow, as if they were being projected onto an enormous, imaginary screen for all to see.

I turned and found no one but an elderly woman behind me. It must have been she who was envious of me. I looked her over. A small woman in a drab outfit, with salt-and-pepper hair, she had something about her that commanded respect. Staring at her perplexedly, I wondered for what she could envy me — someone who had just finished a graveyard shift, with weariness written all over her face.

"Yes, I envy your age and the youthfulness of you both," she said, with a gentle sweep of her hand to encircle me and my son, now shrinking to a little speck as he trotted further into the distance. "I would give all I have acquired for going back to your age."

To this day, I don't know who she was and what she meant by all that she had acquired. I am grateful to her though, for letting me know what I had was most precious. Too often we envy others, being oblivious to what we have that is most precious, till we lose it without knowing. Humanity is a perennial river, flowing on ceaselessly, each of us having all those who are either older or younger than we are before or behind us. We each possess what is the most precious to us; something that no one can take away from us. Do not fret over the encroaching twilight of youth or the dawn of senility. Let your youthfulness shine as long as you live. The only thing that may dim its radiance will be your own admission that you are young no more.

So, to all my friends who have yet to become old: do not envy others; remember it is they who envy you.

鞋

先有了脚，然后才有了鞋。幼小的时候光着脚在地上走，感受沙的温热、草的润凉，那种无拘无束的洒脱与快乐，一生中会将我们从梦中反复唤醒。

走的路远了，便有了跋涉的痛苦。在炎热的沙漠被炙得像鸵鸟一般奔跑，在深陷的沼泽被水蛭蜇出肿痛……

人生是一条无涯的路，于是，人们创造了鞋。

穿鞋是为了赶路，但路上的千难万险，有时尚不如鞋中的一粒沙石令人感到难言的苦痛。鞋，就成了文明人类祖祖辈辈流传的话题。

鞋可由各式各样的原料制成。最简陋的是一片新鲜的芭蕉叶，最昂贵的是仙女留给灰姑娘的那只水晶鞋。

不论什么鞋，最重要的是合脚。

切莫只贪图鞋的华贵，而委屈了自己的脚。别人看到的是鞋，自己感受到的是脚。脚比鞋重要，这是一条真理，许许多多的人却常常忘记。

我做过许多年医生，常给年轻的女孩子包脚，锋利的鞋帮将她们的脚踝"砍"得鲜血淋漓。缠上雪白的纱布，套好光洁的丝袜，她们袅袅地走了。但我知道，当翩翩起舞之时，也许有人会冷不防地抽搐嘴角，那是因为她的鞋。

看到过祖母的鞋，没有看到过祖母的脚。她从不让我们看她的脚，好像那是一件秽物。脚驮着我们站立行走。脚是无辜的，脚是功臣。丑恶的是那鞋，那是一副刑具，一套铸造畸形、残害天性的模型。

每当我看到包办而蒙昧的婚姻，就想到祖母的三寸金莲。

幼时我有一双美丽的红皮鞋，但我很讨厌穿它，就像鞋窝里潜伏着一只夹脚趾的"虫"。每当我不愿穿红皮鞋时，大人们总把手伸进去胡乱一探，然后说，多么好的鞋，快穿上吧！为了不穿这双鞋，我进行了一个孩子所能爆发的最激烈反抗。我始终不明白：一双鞋好不好，为什么不是穿鞋的人具有最后的决定权？

滑冰要穿冰鞋，雪地要着雪靴，下雨要有雨鞋，旅游要有旅游鞋。大千世界，有无数种可供我们挑选的鞋，脚却只有一双。朋友，你可要慎重！

少时参加运动会，临赛的前一天，老师突然给我提来一双橘红色的带钉跑鞋，祝愿我在田径比赛中如虎添翼。我脱下平日训练的白网球鞋，穿上像橘皮一样柔软的跑鞋，心中的自信突然溜掉了。鞋钉将跑道扎出一溜齿痕，我觉得自己的脚被人换成了蹄子。我说我不穿跑鞋，所有的人都说我太傻。发令枪响了，我穿着跑鞋跑完全程。当我习惯性地挺起前胸去撞冲刺线的时候，那根线早已像绶带似的悬挂在别人的胸前。

橘红色的跑鞋无罪，该负责任的是那些劝说我的人。世上有很多很好的鞋，但要看适不适合你的脚。在这里，所有的经验之谈都无济于事，你只需在半夜时分，倾听你自己脚的感觉。

看到好几位赤着脚参加世界田径大赛的南非女子的风采，我报以会心一笑：没有鞋也一样能破世界纪录！脚会长，鞋却不变，于是鞋与脚，就成为一对永恒的矛盾。鞋与脚的力量，究竟谁的更大一些？我想是脚。只见有磨穿了的鞋，没有磨薄了的脚。鞋要束缚脚的时候，脚趾就把鞋面挑开一个洞，到外面凉快去。

脚终有不长的时候，那就是我们开始成熟的年龄。认真地选择一种适合自己的鞋吧！一只脚是男人，一只脚是女人，鞋把他们联结为相似而又绝不相同的一双。从此，世人在人生的旅途上，看到的就不再是脚印，而是鞋印了。

削足适履是一种愚人的残酷，郑人买履是一种智者的迂腐，步履维艰时，鞋与脚要精诚团结；平步青云时，切不要将鞋儿抛弃……

当然，脚比鞋贵重。当鞋确实伤害了脚，我们不妨赤脚赶路！

Shoes

First there were feet, and then came the shoes.

As a child, I would walk about in my bare feet, enjoying the warmth of the sand and the cool of the grass — totally uninhibited — the kind of memory that would last a lifetime, and wake us up again and again in our dreams.

But as we cover the miles, the pain of walking made itself felt — forced to run, like an ostrich under the blazing sun, stung by leeches when mired in a bog, ending up with swellings.

Life is an unending road. Ultimately, people invented the shoes.

Shoes are made for walking and the roads are fraught with

danger.

Sometimes a mere pebble could cause unspeakable pain.

Thus, the shoe became a topic that has been passed down through generations of the civilized human race.

Shoes can be made of vastly different materials. One of the simplest is a sheet of fresh lotus leaf, the most expensive variety being the pair of crystal slippers that the Fairy godmother had left for the little girl covered in cinders.

Now, about the shoes, no matter how fancy the make, it is imperative that they fit. On no account indulge in expensive gadgets at the expense of the comfort of your feet. Other people see the shoes only, but you are feeling it out with your own feet. Feet are more important than shoes. This is a truth that is often forgotten.

I had been a doctor for many years, and had often wrapped up the feet of young girls. The stiff sides of their shoes would often cut into the sides of their ankles and cause bleeding. I would wrap up the wound with white gauze and pull up the silk stockings and walk briskly away. But when they floated away on the dance floor, sometimes they would wince, and I knew that it was because of their shoes.

I had seen my grandma's shoes, but never her feet. She would never show us her feet as if they were something unclean. Our feet support us in standing up and in walking. They're innocent, like a hero. It is the shoes that are unclean — a bizarre man-made instrument of torture, designed to destroy nature.

Whenever I come across an arranged marriage, it would remind me of my grandma's "three-inch lotus feet."

Feet, however, does not allow shoes to squeeze your toes. To the outsider, it is just a pair of shoes, but it is you and you only, that feel it on your feet. In a word, Feet are more important than the shoes.

When a child, I had a beautiful pair of red leather shoes, but I rarely wore it, as if an insect inside would be squeezing my toes. Whenever

I refused to wear that pair of shoes, one of my elders would stick a hand inside and exclaim: "What wonderful shoes? Put them on quick!" To avoid putting on that pair of shoes, I had resorted to all the modes of violent resistance available to a child. I could never make them understand why I the wearer, and no one else, had the right to decide if the shoes fit.

Skates are for skating, snow boots are for snow days, rain boots for rainy days, and sneakers for walking ... In this wide world of ours, there are endless kinds of shoes for us to choose from. But we are equipped with only one pair of feet. Make sure you choose carefully!

I remember once when I was a kid, right on the eve of a sports event, my teacher brought me a pair of orange-coloured running shoes with nails on the soles, wishing me good luck at the field and track. I took off my white sports shoes and put on the pair of orange-coloured running shoes and suddenly my self-confidence evaporated. My spiked shoes left a trail of dents on the ground. I felt my feet being turned into animal hoofs.

I said that I was not going to wear running shoes, and

people around me said that I was being silly. Right then, a shot ran out and I ran down the tract in those running shoes.

I puffed up my chest, according to past practice, to hit the finishing line for the grand finale. But the line was already hanging on someone else' chest — the winner's prize.

The orange-coloured running shoes were not to blame. It was the people who had urged me to wear them, they were to blame. There are countless pairs of good shoes in the world — the problem being which pair is right for you.

Other people's experience is not the answer. All you can do is wait until midnight and listen to the sound of your own feet and find out how they are feeling.

I smiled when seeing bare-footed women athletes from South Africa competing at a world track-and-field event, reassured that being shoeless would not stop them from breaking world records. Shoes and feet are in perpetual conflict — the latter may grow while the former won't. Which are stronger, shoes or feet? I would rather root for feet. I have seen shoes with soles completely worn through, but never a foot made thinner because of walking. If your toes are not snug and feel constrained, they will poke holes through the top of your shoes.

Our feet stop growing as we reach maturity. Choose shoes wisely so that they truly fit. A pair of shoes are like a man and a woman joined in wedlock, similar but never identical, leaving matching prints not of bare feet, but cushioning soles of shoes.

Chinese idioms that refer to shoes abound, such as "reshaping one's feet to fit into new shoes," which connotes sheer stupidity, or "A man of the Zheng State buying his shoes" that describes stubborn dogmatism. In the same spirit, we can say that an arduous trek requires truly fitting shoes. When you are ebullient in success, don't forget the humble footgear that has helped to get you there. Also, be resolute to shed the ones that are hurting your feet.

没有一棵小草自惭形秽

被人邀请去看一棵树，一棵古老的树。大约有五千年的历史，已被唐朝的地震弯折了腰，半匍匐着，依然不倒，享受着人们尊敬的注视。

我混在人群中直着脖子虔诚地仰望着古树顶端稀疏的绿叶，一边想，人和树相比是多么的渺小啊。人生出来，肯定是比一粒树种要大很多倍，但人没法长得如树般伟岸。在树小的时候，人是很容易就把树枝包括树干折断，甚至把树连根拔起，树就结束了生命。就算是小树长成了大树，归宿也是被人伐了去，修成各种各样实用的物件。长得好的树，花纹美丽木质出众，也像美女一样，红颜薄命，被人劫掠的可能性更大，于是很多珍贵的树种濒临灭绝。在这一点上，树是不如人的。美女可以人造，树却是不可以人造的。

树比人活得长久，只要假以天年，人是绝对活不过一棵树的。树并不以此傲人，爷爷种下的树，照样以累累果实报答那人的孙子或是其他人的后代。

通常情况下，树是绝对不伤人的。即便如前几天报上所载一些村民在树下避雨，遭了雷击致死，那元凶也不是树，而是闪电，树也是受害者。人却是绝对伤树的，地球上森林数量的锐减就是明证，人成了树的天敌。

树比人坚忍。在人不能居住的地方，树却裸身生长着，不需要炉火或是空调的保护。树会帮助人的，在饥馑的时候，人扒过树的皮以充饥，我们却从未听到过树会扒下人的什么零件的传闻。

很多书籍记载过这棵古树，若是在树群里评选名人的话，这棵古树是一定名列前茅了。很多诗人词人咏颂过这棵古树，如果树把那些词句都当作叶子一般披挂起来，一定不堪重负。唐朝的地震不曾把它压倒，这些赞美会让它扑在地上。

树的寿命是如此长久，居然看到过妲己那个朝代的事情。在我们死后很多年，这棵古树还会枝叶繁茂地生长着。一想到这一点，无边的嫉妒就转成深深的自卑。作为一个人活不了那么久远，伤感让我低下头来，于是我就看到了一棵小草，一棵长在古树之旁的小草。只有细长的两三片叶子，纤细得如同婴儿的睫毛。树叶缝隙的阳光打在草叶的几丝脉络上，再落到地上，阳光变得如绿纱一样飘浮了。

这样一株柔弱的小草，在这样一棵神圣的树底下，一定该俯首称臣毕恭毕敬了吧？我竭力想从小草身上找出低眉顺眼的谦卑，最后以失望告终。这棵不知名的小草，毫无疑问是非常渺小的。就寿命计算，假设一岁一枯荣，古树很可能见过小草五千辈以前的祖先。就体量计算，古树抵得过千百万小草集合而成的大军。就价值来说，人们千里万里路地赶了来，只为瞻仰古树，我敢肯定，没有一个人是为了探望小草。

既然我作为一个人，都在古树面前自惭形秽了，小草你怎能不顶礼膜拜？我这样想着，就蹲下来看着小草。在这样一棵历史久远、声名卓著的古树身边为邻，你岂不要羞愧死了？

小草昂然立着，我向它吐了一口气，它就被吹得蜷曲了身子，但我气息一尽，它就像弹簧般伸展了叶脉，快乐地抖动着。我再吹一口气，它还是在弯曲之后怡然挺立。我悲哀地发现，不停地吹下去，有我气绝倒地的一刻，小草却安然。

草是卑微的，但卑微并非指向羞惭。在庄严的大树身旁，一棵微不足道的小草都可以毫不自惭形秽地生活着，何况我们万物灵长的人类！

Even the Humble Grass Has Dignity

I was once invited to see an ancient tree, with an age of about five thousand years. Stunted by an earthquake sometime during the Tang Dynasty (AD 618–907), and half stooping since, it stood majestic, inspiring awe in all who came to pay its homage.

Shuffling in a throng of visitors, I craned my neck and looked up at the apex of the ancient tree with its thinning canopy. I couldn't help thinking how minuscule a human is in comparison. Although a newborn is umpteen times the size of a tree seed, the infant will never reach the towering height of a tree. Yet, humans can be destructive. A sapling, weak and feeble, can be broken in half or uprooted by the force of a human hand. Even if it is spared such a fate and grows to its full height, it may still end up being logged and made into practical items of one kind or another. Some tree species, with prized grain textures, are prone to being targeted by harvesters, short-lived like ill-fated beauties. Many precious species are thus driven to the brink of extinction. They suffer worse fate than human beauties that can be copiously reproduced.

Yet, trees naturally live longer than people. If they are allowed to live to a ripe old age, no human can be a match. Yet trees are humble and generous. A fruit tree planted by one's or someone else's grandfather, can still be bearing fruits.

Trees don't normally harm people. Even when someone is struck by lightning when standing under a tree in a thunderstorm, as it is sometimes reported in the news, the culprit is never the tree but the thunderbolt. The tree can be a victim, too. People, on the other hand, do harm trees. The sharp decline of forest cover on earth is the unequivocal proof that humans are trees' natural nemesis.

Trees are tougher than humans. They can thrive in areas utterly inhospitable to humanity, without the comfort of hearth or air-conditioning that humans relish. Trees help people, too. In times of famine, hungry souls chewed shreds of bark after pulling them off trees to quell their hunger. Yet we have yet to hear trees pulling off appendages off humans on purpose.

This ancient tree had been referenced in works of classic literature, deservedly a tree celebrity. It had been a source of inspiration for poets of many past eras. If their adulatory verses were to be leaves, the collective weight would have been more than the tree could bear, though it had withstood a major earthquake over a millennium ago.

The tree was so old that it had even witnessed events concerning Daji, the favourite consort of King Zhou of Shang Dynasty, ten centuries before Common Era. It will likely see many more years after we are gone. The thought made me feel both envious and inferior. Downcast, as I pondered on the fickleness of life, my eyes fell on a couple of slender blades of grass at the foot of the rugged ancient tree, delicate as an infant's eyelashes. The sunlight that filtered through the leaves and bounced off the finely textured blades took on a verdant, surreal hue.

Would the humble grass, under such a sacred old tree, show every sign of feebleness and submission? I searched hard, but to no avail. The grass's size is one millionth, and its life span five thousandth, those of the ancient tree. Multitudes of people travel hundreds of miles to pay homage to the tree, but none do so to the grass. How could the feeble grass be not humbled by the ancient tree?

I crouched for a closer look. Still, I did not see any hint of inferiority in the grass with a celebrity tree as its neighbour. The grass stood erect, and its stalk curled slightly in the puff of air I exhaled, but instantly straightened up, swaying merrily, as I stopped puffing. I blew again and it bounced back after curling briefly as before. I found to my chagrin that I could puff my heart out and the grass would still stand unscathed.

The grass is humble, yet humbleness is not equivalent to shame. Next to a giant of a tree, a grass can live proudly without self-loathing. Why don't we humans, the smartest of all living things?